Embodying Diversity

Identity, (Bio)Diversity, & Sexuality

Gay Men's Issues in Religious Studies Series
Volume 6

Proceedings of the
Gay Men's Issues in Religion Group
of the American Academy of Religion
Washington, DC
Fall 1993

Essays by
Julie Byrne
J. Michael Clark
Robin Gorsline
Ronald E. Long
Daniel T. Spencer

Edited by
J. Michael Clark &
Michael L. Stemmeler

Las Colinas
Monument Press
1995

Published by
Monument Press
Las Colinas, Texas

Library of Congress Cataloging-in-Publication Data

Embodying diversity : identity, (bio)diversity & sexuality / essays by Julie Byrne . . . [et al.] ; edited by J. Michael Clark & Michael L. Stemmeler.

p. cm. -- (Gay men's issues in religious studies series ; v. 6)

"Proceedings of the Gay Men's Issues in Religion Group of the American Academy of Religion, San Francisco, CA, Fall 1993."

Includes bibliographical references.

ISBN 0-930383-44-3 (pbk.)

1. Homosexuality--Religious aspects--Christianity--Congresses. 2. Gay men--Religious life--Congresses. 3. Gay men--Sexual ethics--Congresses. 4. Gays--Identity--Congresses. 5. Sexual ethics--Congresses. 6. Religious ethics--Congresses. I. Byrne, Julie, 1968- . II. Clark, J. Michael (John Michael), 1953- . III. Stemmeler, Michael L., 1955- . IV. American Academy of Religion. Gay Men's Issues in Religion Group. V. Series.
BR115.H6E4 1995
291.1'7835766--dc20

95-37419
CIP

Table of Contents

Preface: On Coming Full Circle

The concept of a *Gay Men's Issues in Religious Studies* book series developed simultaneously with the inauguration of the Gay Men's Issues in Religion program unit of the American Academy of Religion (AAR). As a group of us met informally during the 1987 Boston meetings, Michael Stemmeler, then a doctoral candidate at Temple University, now on the faculty at Central Michigan University, agreed to be my co-chair for the emerging group and my co-editor for our published volumes. We shared concerns that our work not be restricted merely to presentations at the annual AAR meetings. We were also very much aware of the difficulties facing openly gay male scholars seeking publication and wanted to ensure that our work find a wider audience; this book series has provided the forum not then available for both our actual presentations and the available completed papers not actually presented due to time constraints. The papers from our inaugural meeting in Chicago in 1988 constituted our first volume, published in 1990.

While our publishing schedule has been sporadic, given our authors' obligations, Dr. Stemmeler and myself, along with one guest editor and our numerous presenters over the years, have provided in the now six volumes of the series all the work of our program unit during our tenure as the group's co-chairs. After our initial probationary two-year term as a "consultation" (1988, 1989) the Gay Men's Issues in Religion Group assumed a more integral role in the AAR with a five-year term beginning in 1990. According to

AAR rules, co-chairs must step down after six years; consequently, Dr. Stemmeler cycled onto the group steering committee following the 1993 meeting and I became an informal consulting "co-chair emeritus" if you will. Our new leadership team of Drs. Robert Goss and Mark Kowalewski began their coordinating work for the group in 1994, winning the group a second five-year term, beginning in 1995.

The papers in this sixth volume developed from the presentations of that last annual meeting during which Dr. Stemmeler and I served as co-chairs, our 1993 meeting in Washington, DC. These papers represent the coming full circle of our work during our first six years as an AAR program unit. Developing gay theology during this period has increasingly become embodied, experiential, and immanental. Consistent with that development, Julie Byrne's article herein examines the spirituality and (sub)culture of African American transvestites in New York City; Ron Long articulates what is becoming his signature sexual theology; and, I attempt to take our work beyond the gay male ghetto toward an ecological perspective which fundamentally reshapes eschatology. Finally, Robin Gorsline and Dan Spencer revisit a conversation begun in our previous volume, assuring the continuation of an ongoing dialogue with our lesbian colleagues. While the future work of the Gay Men's Issues in Religion Group now depends upon new leadership, those of us involved in its first six years and these six volumes sincerely hope our readers will find nurturing food for thought in these pages. I also offer a heartfelt thanks to my colleague Michael Stemmeler for his many efforts on our behalf these six plus years.

-J. Michael Clark, *Summer Solstice 1995*

Julie Byrne

Identity Goes Up in Flames:
Gay Ethics, Deleuze & Guattari, & *Paris is Burning*

1. Introduction:
Paris is Burning & the Limits of Identity Politics

In the four years since its release, *Paris is Burning*,[1] Jennie Livingston's 1989 documentary film of black drag queen subculture in New York City, has become a classic of gay iconography.[2] The documentary records the lives of members of "families" of mostly non-white gay men which have been springing up on the streets of New York City since the 1960s. Many of the men are runaways from homes and parents who rejected them for being gay; many of them hustle or steal to scrape together money for rent and food. The family members range in age from the 13-year-old interviewed on the street at 3 a.m. to the *grande dame* Dorian Corey in her dressing room, who remembers without nostalgia the developments in queen fashion since the old days of the '60s. The families together comprise a world where "being gay is one hundred percent right," says one interviewee.

The most meaningful rituals in this world are the costume balls, sponsored periodically by various families, or Houses. Members of the Houses, called "children" no matter what their age, walk in the mode of runway models in various categories of dress, the object being to be more "real" in whatever the chosen category than rivals in other families. The children live for the balls. Pepper Labeija, mother of the House of Labeija, tells us that the children often go hungry rather than suffer the humiliation of passé attire at a ball.

Gay-attuned movie-goers and critics have commented extensively on the multiply difficult social positions of the *Paris is Burning* queens, namely, their triple identities as black, gay and queen; their economic marginalization; their formation of alternative social structures; their creation of the fantasy world of the costume balls; and, most recently, the disintegration of their subculture due to violence, fame and AIDS.[3] Almost all writers on the film have assumed that the difficult aspects of the subculture's social position have to do with its members' problematic identities, and, given the film's important exploration of cross-dressing and transsexuality, they are amply justified in their assumptions. Identity--its formation, affirmation, transference and loss--is a reasonable way to organize interpretation of the film. For in the American liberal tradition, to have identity--to be recognized as an individual in pursuit of life, liberty and happiness--integrally comprises the well-being of the nation's citizens.

On the one hand, I recognize with most critics that the queens of *Paris is Burning* are engaged in some profound identity struggles. At some level, it is true to say that they are denied identity, that they are not happy with the identities they were "given," or that the ones they want are unattainable. But on the other hand, some clues to their lives provided in the film make me want to resist an interpretation organized around the concept of identity. After all, identity as a concept has not existed since time immemorial; it belongs to a particular historical configuration of ideas dating to eighteenth-century Enlightenment political thinkers. Invoking the concept of identity necessarily calls forth a nexus of other ideas tied up with identity, such as the individual, the state, law, rights and democracy--all of which, together, comprise liberal democratic philosophy.[4] In other words, apart from the context of liberal democratic philosophy, the concept of identity makes no sense.

a. The Liberal Democratic Context of Identity Politics

While identity lends power to the interpretation of some aspects of *Paris is Burning*, its embeddedness in liberal democratic philosophy poses urgent problems. To be precise, liberal democracies make only "identities," but no other conception of fulfilled lives, available. Certain parts of *Paris is Burning*, which I will explore in depth later, suggest that the wildly off-center position of the black drag queen subculture places this subculture in some largely unrecognized, barely recognizable relationship to identity and to the institutions of liberal democracy. This unrecognized relationship, I will argue, ignores or disrupts the usual dialectic relationship in liberal democracy between the individual and the state, in which the state sanctions certain identities and people forge identities to fight for state recognition. Instead, in this different *adialectical* stance of the queens toward the state, the queens seem to ignore the state altogether, and in their diffidence, deeply trouble the state in small and large ways. The drag queens' attitudes often resemble nothing that the liberal framework can accommodate without consigning them to realms of delusion, escapism and insanity. Yet their lives also model one particularly vigorous alternative to liberal ethics. Why we need an alternative to liberal ethics, and how the queens of *Paris is Burning* help provide that altenative, I shall endeavor to show in the following pages.

b. Deleuze & Guattari in Defense of Unidentifiability

In an attempt to understand in more detail what forces could constitute the sort of unidentifiable, adialectic group emergent in *Paris is Burning*, I will make use of the work of French thinkers Gilles Deleuze and Félix Guattari (referred to in shorthand as D&G). Deleuze, a philosopher who has been writing since the 1960s, and Guattari, a radical psychoanalyst and political activist, have made it their business in two collaborative books--*Anti-Oedipus*, first published in France in 1972, and its sequel *A Thousand Plateaus*, published in 1980, both part of a project they called *Capitalism and Schizophrenia*[5]--to rescue from obscurity just these sorts of adialectic, unidentifiable groups. In *Anti-Oedipus*, the recalled or remembered group is *schizophrenics*, defined not by the disease schizophrenia, but by their resistance to restrictive, Oedipally-fixated psychoanalysis.[6]

In *A Thousand Plateaus*, D&G turn their attention to remembering what they call *nomad groups*. Groups that come to mind when we think of nomads include Tuaregs, Mongols and Native Americans; anthropologically, these groups are characterized predominantly by wandering movement, rather than movement within a fixed location or movement from point to point. While retaining the association of nomads with wandering, D&G expand the anthropological definition of nomads to include any groups that move like nomads move. Nomads, for their purposes, are groups which ignore geographical lines drawn by states, and which habitually roam as if the markings on maps did not exist.[7] This habitual roaming and aversion to linearity has other implications for nomad social structure, implications to which I will return later. For now, it is enough to say that the nomadic groups described in the "Treatise on Nomadology" in *A Thousand Plateaus*[8] anticipates the social formation of the black drag queen subculture of *Paris is Burning* in fascinating ways. The "Treatise" will serve as the reference text for the alternative to liberal ethics this paper proposes.

In sum, I hope to read *Paris is Burning* as a possible site of a gay ethics not affiliated with identity politics, but rather with an adialectic activism described by Deleuze and Guattari in the "Treatise on Nomadology." This reading is not intended to supplant various interpretations of the film in terms of identity politics, interpretations which I consider crucial to any understanding of the film's political and aesthetic resonance. My reading is intended, however, to argue that limiting one's hermeneutics to the concept of identity will obscure the queens' radicality, and that utilizing the particular alternative hermeneutic provided by Deleuze and Guattari's provocative account of nomads expands the range of resources available for gay living.

The reader will have to wait some time before reaching my full analysis of *Paris is Burning*, for I will take two detours, backtracking over terrain I have covered all too briefly to this point. The detours will take me first through a quick sketch of gay ethics in the last fifteen years, and second, through a short discussion of the liberal democratic ideology that, I will argue, has sustained recent gay ethics. From there I will outline D&G's general project, which obliquely criticizes identity politics and develops an alternative ethic to address some of its problems. Finally taking up the "Treatise on Nomadology," my reading of *Paris is Burning* will intersect a few of the multivalent intimations of D&G's alternative ethics, fleshing out one powerful untapped version of gay living.

2. Gay Ethics in the Liberal Democratic Context

My first order of business, then, will be to sketch briefly my understanding of what has recently counted as ethics in gay communities. We do not need to be reminded that throughout the 1980s, the AIDS crisis has dominated much of what has been understood as gay ethics. Though to say that AIDS-response politics and gay ethics are the same thing would criminally reduce the range of gay theoretical, artistic and spiritual endeavor of the last decade (not to mention the last several millennia) to a fraction of its scope, the threats AIDS has posed to gay populations have unified and intensified gay activism.

In the early 1980s, AIDS made imperative a mutual engagement--for the first time in United States history--between those invested in gay life and the public institutions of the country. If AIDS is certainly a natural catastrophe of massive proportions, that's not the half of it. The manipulation of AIDS by this liberal democracy, as gay activists saw very quickly, has proved a far deadlier force than "nature." Like the "airborne toxic event" of Don DeLillo's novel *White Noise*,[9] AIDS as constructed and bandied about by majoritarian social structures--media, the medical establishment, legislators, Hollywood, educators-- threatened to multiply its already formidable dangers to include the legally sanctioned disintegration of gay communities and near-genocidal excuses for bigotry.

The dimensions of the AIDS crisis set gay politics in the United States on a newfound and decidedly liberal-democratic track. For purposes of securing information, health care, civil rights and legal recourse, gay groups started talking to state institutions, bargaining with them, protesting against them--and vice versa. If the many lifestyles called gay could not fifteen years ago have been gathered under one umbrella for any reason, if much of what had been elemental to gay politics and aesthetics specifically *resisted* identification and identifiability, if gay communities cultivated their underground status partly in fear but partly in anti-establishment glee, now gay survival demanded engagement with the resources of liberal democracy.

In short, the continuity of gay communities depended upon their success in claiming the rights of individuals on the terms provided by this liberal democracy. Unsurprisingly to gay-attuned folks, the humor, athleticism and creativity with which gay communities have stormed the arena of rights claimants have surpassed the wildest expectations of what fun was possible with liberal democracy. The 1993 national gay rights march in Washington, D. C. was called by organizers a "civil rights mingle," capturing at once its dual function as politics and party.[10] In my home state of North Carolina, when the state chapter of Act-Up fitted a huge condom on Jesse Helms' Raleigh home, or when choreographer Ron Brown's 1993 American Dance Festival class performed his moving AIDS deathwatch piece, "Combat Review/Guard Duty," they reimagined for their audiences the powers of social protest. Colorful Act-Up protests and brilliant artists like Brown are but two examples of the explosive national gay activist movement.

In sum, the engagement of gay politics with the opportunities of liberal democracy has made monumental strides towards gay liberation. I have no intention of romanticizing the oppression of the closet with my blithe references to its "aesthetic of unidentifiability" and "anti-establishment glee," nor will I suggest that the gay activist engagement with liberal democracy was misguided from the start and must be trashed in favor of some new program. As Deleuze and Guattari are careful to say in their various writings, what is proposed here is "Not better, just different."[11]

But what troubles me is our frequent habit, as thinkers used to the terms of identity politics, of translating what is different to the same familiar terms, of seeing all lives in "identical" terms. If there are certain pressing disadvantages of the identity politics version of gay activism, different activisms--scuttled to forgotten places such as the black drag queen ghetto of *Paris is Burning*--must be recovered in different terms. Only then can these different activisms hold out possibilities of compromising less and promising more for the future of gay lives.

3. The Costs of Gay Identity

At this point, in a second detour on the way to Paris, I need to make plain these pressing disadvantages of the liberal democratic model of gay activism, discussing quickly what I mean by liberal democracy, and where I think its weaknesses lie. Liberal democracy refers to Enlightenment political thinkers' blend of "democracy," revived from antiquity, and "liberalism," the then-new anthropology of free and equal citizens of the state. Grounding this nation's constitution, liberal democracy is supposed to work like this: there is something called the "individual" or "citizen" who has "rights" and claims them from the "state" on the basis of her or his membership in something called "universal humanity," with the assumption that when every individual's inalienable rights are respected, citizens will attain the utopia of social harmony. Liberal democracy involves talking between the individual and the state, a *dia-*

lectic: Either the citizen or the state can initiate a dialogue in which things are offered, refused and bargained for.

This dialectic between the state and the individual (or group *of individuals*) provides a democratic forum for compromise over political and material capital, and need not be sinister. In many cases, groups which have found themselves isolated and oppressed understand the things they compromise as a small price to pay for the political power gained and the exhilaration of connection with other groups and institutions. For example, as I have noted, in the case of gay identity politics, engagement with the resources of liberal democracy has proved overwhelmingly successful and brilliantly liberating for thousands.

a. Identity Endowed by the State

So, if liberalism has proved so conducive to gay liberation, why am I even bothering to suggest an alternative? For several reasons. First, state recognition of gay identity does not come free. Our liberal democratic constitution would have us believe that identity is a natural, pre-existent component of human beings which states are kind enough to organize for us. But the other side of the coin needs remembering: identity is recognized--perhaps even constructed--by the state so that the state will have subjects to govern. The political clout of identity politics derives not from its particular aptness to articulate gay experiences, but rather from the liberal democratic ideology that materializes identity as such and grants it, at the price of certain conformities, to its constituents.

This radical critique of liberal democracy--mounted in other forms in theological and philosophical circles by ethicists such as Stanley Hauerwas and Alisdair MacIntyre--goes several steps further. If liberal democracy does not merely beneficently organize pre-existent individuals, but actually *invents* the idea of individuals to maintain a steady base of jurisdiction, then this means that the dialectic between individual and state always ultimately benefits the state. Regardless of the friendliness or vitriol of the dialectic, if the state got the individual to talk, he's already half won over. In other words, individuals who find themselves compelled to engage in dialogue with a state have already been in large part constituted by that state, and will continue to compromise some interests in exchange for political capital available from the state. "Identity," that word that has figured so largely in gay politics of the last fifteen years, is but one example of an item of political capital up for negotiation in the dialectic, capital which the state rewards only to those who are already "on the state's side," that is, who display the characteristics of the well-legislated, well-regulated individual.

It will be argued that I have tied identity too closely with state recognition. Surely, one might say, if gay identity politics has accomplished anything, it has successfully undermined conventional definitions of identity and expanded notions of what counts as identity. As Richard Goldstein writes in the *Village Voice*, "No sooner did the gay community secure the right to exist ... than it began to deviate from all the models that had been devised."[12] This is true, but the liberal democratic machinery of these United States accommodates expanding notions of identity fairly well. Its built-in provisions for social protest make it an ingeniously flexible system. The problem for gay activists who worry about restriction is not whether this state can accommodate their new notions of identity, but rather, whether there is anything this state *cannot* accommodate. Is it possible *not* to talk with the state? Can a group elude its encodements? If not, a discussion of the ethics of identity politics becomes meaningless.

Fortunately, the state has not, and I believe cannot, succeed in encoding everything for its easy inventories. Although liberal democracy is characterized by flexibility to the point of near-totalitarianism, its expansive dialectical playing field nevertheless permits some moves and disallows others. For example, a rights-claiming group cannot rob from the rich and give to the poor, because property figures centrally in liberal democratic law. A group cannot proclaim the immanent end of the world and still profit from the game, because while scientific claims are encouraged, faith claims are not. A group cannot realize its goals "by any means necessary," because if verbal terrorism is permitted, armed terrorism is not. A group cannot expect state support if it is a group of separatist anarchists, for utopias other than national social harmony are not allowed.

Of course, many good citizens are not bothered that the likes of Robin Hood, David Koresh, Malcolm X and the Grateful Deadheads don't get their full slices of American pie. I, for different reasons, am likewise encouraged that they don't. It means that even our miraculously malleable liberal democracy cannot accommodate and neutralize all weirdnesses--and we are a more ethical society for it. Weird groups know what they're doing. They know that if they play the liberal democratic game, they will already have lost some of the distinctiveness that marginalized them in the first place; they will have delimited the ways they can desire to live. They also know that in retreating from the liberal democratic playing field, they relinquish rights to the spoils.

b. Identity & Convention, Victimology, & Fascism

There are second, third and fourth ethical reasons why I am challenging the largely successful political alliance of the gay movement with the structures of liberal democracy--reasons which are a lot briefer. For one, it seems to me better to have several ways to think about human lives rather than one way, especially if that one way seems to be the favorite of the folks who have the most money and power. Identity politics will never fundamentally challenge the status quo, because people in positions of power all agree with its suppositions. Is it a problem that the status quo is not challenged? Richard Rorty says, no. In my opinion, yes. Paraphrasing philosopher Michel Foucault, I think the liberal democratic system that has dealt so much oppression to so many groups has not merely gone wrong a couple times; instead, it might be time to suppose that the liberal democratic system *always* oppresses *somebody*, as part of its functioning.[13]

The third reason, closely related to the first, to be concerned about a successful alliance between gay groups and liberal democracy lies in my deepening suspicion that the claim to status as victim launches and permeates identity politics. In order to valorize gay identity one must first have absorbed the notion that the gay identity needs valorizing, that gay identity has been oppressed. The potential political and psychological damage of this victim claim has only begun to be explored, in disreputable corners of academia, for instance, in the case of feminism, by Camille Paglia or Katie Roiphe, or in the case of race studies, by Shelby Steele. Claiming gay victimization, it might be argued, damagingly allows the majority to neutralize gay challenges, because the majority is not threatened by victims; or it might allow all victims to place themselves in a flat category undifferentiated by race, class, gender, sexual preference and other variables; or it might encourage the very passivity or abnegation of responsibility that activist politics is supposed to dispel.

The fourth and final reason why I suggest that gay politics at its peril owes all its force conceptualizations of identity is that no one is an identity all the time. Paraphrasing Denise Riley, I would say that "it's not possible to live twenty-four hours a day soaked in the immediate awareness of" one's sexual orientation, that consciousness of one's sexual orientation "has, mercifully, a flickering nature."[14] If all of us think and desire differently from our identities at times, the loyalty required by gay--or lesbian, or feminist, or Asian--identification is exacted at the price of other equally valid, sometimes more desirable ways of organizing our lives. And when one identification simply replaces another, political resistance has only led back to square one.

That is to say, a group that understands playing by the rules of liberal democracy to be the *only* political option has ceased to set its own terms of desire. Not only has such a group ceased to set its own terms; it has ceased to remember or recognize the existence of groups who have fled the liberal democratic playing field, who have decided that the desires allowed by the liberal framework no longer satisfy, that attainable goods only promise further compromises. Let me return after this detour to the black drag queen ghetto. The *Paris is Burning* subculture exemplifies one such group fleeing the playing field of liberal democracy. That is why a reading of *Paris is Burning* exclusively through the vocabulary of identity politics will miss its heterodoxical clues and radical quirks. But I attempt this reading of *Paris is Burning* not only to recuperate what I see as a more modulated and respectful understanding of the drag queens' lives; I do it also to recover a more modulated and respectful understanding of all our lives. After all, anthropologizing any group always says more about the person analyzing than the people analyzed.

To set up the framework for this reading, I turn now to a general introduction to Deleuze and Guattari, courtesy of their friend Michel Foucault.

3. Deleuze & Guattari's Models of Unidentifiability

The French philosopher Michel Foucault is a more familiar figure in gay political and intellectual circles than Deleuze and Guattari; his books have been available longer in English translation, and he spent considerable amounts of time in the United States. Foucault's social histories on the birth of modern institutions, which theorize how institutions create the subjects of their own jurisdiction, have contributed massively to the critique of liberal democracy laid out above. For example, in *Discipline and Punish*, Foucault refutes the liberal supposition that criminals existed before there were prisons to control them, demonstrating conversely that prisons actually invent and maintain criminals.[15]

By way of introduction, I mention that philosophers Foucault and Deleuze were friends and mutual admirers. Deleuze wrote a near-hagiographic book on Foucault,[16] and Foucault wrote the preface to *Anti-Oedipus.* Hailing *Anti-Oedipus* in one interview as "an event" which "has no other source of reference than its own prodigious theoretical inventiveness,"[17] Foucault writes in his preface that the text amounts to "(may its authors forgive me) a book of ethics, the first book of ethics to be written in France in quite a long time." The word "ethics" is startling in a book of poststructuralist philosophy, but Foucault uses it quite deliberately. I will return to this point later in the discussion.

Foucault continues in his preface with the best short introduction to the work of Deleuze and Guattari that I can provide. It summarizes the two-volume *Capitalism and Schizophrenia* philosophical project of replacing dualism with multiplicities; freeing desire from its representation; warning of the dangers of state-engaged political action; and, recommending kinds of action unaffiliated with majoritarian power structures. D&G's entire philosophical project is driven by a sense of the urgency, which Foucault shares, of imagining different revolutions and understanding the potential limits, even the "fascisms," of the ones we are now practicing. I quote Foucault on *Anti-Oedipus* at length:[18]

> How does one keep from being fascist, even (especially) when one believes oneself to be a revolutionary militant?...
>
> I would summarize [*Anti-Oedipus*] as follows if I were to make this great book into a manual or guide to everyday life:
>
> · Free political action from all unitary and totalizing paranoia.
>
> · Develop action, thought, and desires by proliferation, juxtaposition, and disjunction, not by subdivision and pyramidal hierarchization. ...
>
> · Prefer what is positive and multiple, difference over uniformity, flows over unities, mobile arrangements over systems. Believe that what is productive is not sedentary but nomadic. . . .
>
> · Do not demand of politics that it restore the "rights" of the individual, as philosophy has defined them. The individual is the product of power. What is needed is to "de-individualize" by means of multiplication and displacement, diverse combinations. The group must not be the organic bond uniting hierarchized individuals, but a constant generator of de-individualization.

a. Recovering Alternatives/Lines of Flight

D&G undertake the "de-individualization" of which Foucault speaks by methods of "multiplication and dis-

placement," suggesting ways to see multiple
decision-making situation. There are, D&G
options most political programs offer: work v
or be consigned to total ignominy. But isn
case, D&G ask, that these are merely the onl
the state would like groups to see? In both th
laborative books, D&G criticize radical polit
(including Marxists, feminists, gays, and Fre
don't realize that there are politics beyond
dual/state dialectic, and that it is an ethical oblig
cover and practice those politics. In D&G's te
political activism has been so "overcoded" by st
of desire that what D&G variously call "third"
"lines of flight" from dialectic are barely visible,
imaginable and seem undesirable.

D&G's great impatience lies with the con
lapsing of categories, on the left as well as the ri
recognizable forms of the state-individual dialect
philosophical project constantly rescues from co
these "third" options and "lines of flight." They pil
amples until we realize that every constricted
problem offers not just one third option or a single
flight, but multitudes of other options, infinite
routes. For example, given a choice between two
some candidates for office, you can drive around with
painted on your car, like the one I saw in Durham in
November: "Don't vote for anybody, ever! The go
ment is your enemy!" Or you're a professor up for t
at College X. You don't *have* to win or lose. You
open up a bed-and-breakfast in the mountains.

Single episodes of people taking "third" opt
don't seem like much, but accumulatively they could

resists the Oedipal resumption
"becoming-woman." Some feminis
Deleuze and Guattari to task for w
and even essentialism of this cen
charge of sexism sometimes clings
remarkable tone-deafness to femini
as his essay on masochism[19]), it
given the pair's philosophic co
woman" indulges essentialist tende
concept features less centrally in
sand Plateaus.

But more problematically,
the central process of becoming
quately conveys the *group* nature
here means, of course, not a grou
group more like a storm, a pack or
movement in the same general direc
ways only "partial."[20] D&G themse
duals, they say in the first lines of *A*
a sort of writing pack: "The two of
together. Since each of us was sev
quite a crowd." Such self-erasure, o
to use Foucault's word, aims to reco
formations of lives, taking a "line of
tic choice between individual agen
The strategy aims "[t]o reach, not t
longer says I, but the point where it
portance whether one says I."[21]

"Becoming-woman" is then d
sand Plateaus for the new parad
"becoming-animal," which remedies t
character of the former. Developing

placement," suggesting ways to see multiple options in any decision-making situation. There are, D&G say, only two options most political programs offer: work within the state or be consigned to total ignominy. But isn't it likely the case, D&G ask, that these are merely the only two options the state would like groups to see? In both their major collaborative books, D&G criticize radical political activists (including Marxists, feminists, gays, and Freudians) who don't realize that there are politics beyond the individual/state dialectic, and that it is an ethical obligation to recover and practice those politics. In D&G's terms, radical political activism has been so "overcoded" by state regimes of desire that what D&G variously call "third" options or "lines of flight" from dialectic are barely visible, largely unimaginable and seem undesirable.

D&G's great impatience lies with the constant collapsing of categories, on the left as well as the right, into recognizable forms of the state-individual dialectic; their philosophical project constantly rescues from cooptation these "third" options and "lines of flight." They pile up examples until we realize that every constricted dialectic problem offers not just one third option or a single line of flight, but multitudes of other options, infinite escape routes. For example, given a choice between two loathsome candidates for office, you can drive around with a sign painted on your car, like the one I saw in Durham in early November: "Don't vote for anybody, ever! The government is your enemy!" Or you're a professor up for tenure at College X. You don't *have* to win or lose. You could open up a bed-and-breakfast in the mountains.

Single episodes of people taking "third" options don't seem like much, but accumulatively they could be

poststructuralist philosophy, but Foucault uses it quite deliberately. I will return to this point later in the discussion.

Foucault continues in his preface with the best short introduction to the work of Deleuze and Guattari that I can provide. It summarizes the two-volume *Capitalism and Schizophrenia* philosophical project of replacing dualism with multiplicities; freeing desire from its representation; warning of the dangers of state-engaged political action; and, recommending kinds of action unaffiliated with majoritarian power structures. D&G's entire philosophical project is driven by a sense of the urgency, which Foucault shares, of imagining different revolutions and understanding the potential limits, even the "fascisms," of the ones we are now practicing. I quote Foucault on *Anti-Oedipus* at length:[18]

> How does one keep from being fascist, even (especially) when one believes oneself to be a revolutionary militant?...
>
> I would summarize [*Anti-Oedipus*] as follows if I were to make this great book into a manual or guide to everyday life:
>
> · Free political action from all unitary and totalizing paranoia.
>
> · Develop action, thought, and desires by proliferation, juxtaposition, and disjunction, not by subdivision and pyramidal hierarchization. ...
>
> · Prefer what is positive and multiple, difference over uniformity, flows over unities, mobile arrangements over systems. Believe that what is productive is not sedentary but nomadic. ...
>
> · Do not demand of politics that it restore the "rights" of the individual, as philosophy has defined them. The individual is the product of power. What is needed is to "de-individualize" by means of multiplication and displacement, diverse combinations. The group must not be the organic bond uniting hierarchized individuals, but a constant generator of de-individualization.

a. Recovering Alternatives/Lines of Flight

D&G undertake the "de-individualization" of which Foucault speaks by methods of "multiplication and dis-

radically subversive. To explain how, I will dive into D&G's terminology and hopefully not get us too lost. D&G use a rarified language to convey their concepts, a language intended to perform their understanding of these "lines of flight" or "third" options in revolutionary action. The central process of their philosophy--the process of remembering disallowed desires and recovering sightings of third options --is called in their phraseology "becoming." The concept of "becoming" supplants dialectic models of action by proposing that action need not involve "persons" with "identities" who "do" things, such that the person is separable from the identity and the action. Instead, *action constitutes the person*, whose characteristics never amount to an identity, because she is always acting and becoming something else.

b. Identifying vs. Becoming

Names therefore do not have to do with essences of people or things, but with their movements and speeds and mannerisms. If you name a group, as D&G understand it, you are not *identifying* them, but describing their characteristic ways of *moving*. This categorization by movement rather than by identities produces what Foucault called above "mobile arrangements" rather than "systems." For example, categorizing by movement, a racehorse has more in common with a race-dog than with a plough-horse; similarly, a woman working at Goldman-Sachs has more in common with a man working at Goldman-Sachs than with the woman who cleans her house.

The schizophrenics of *Anti-Oedipus,* as mentioned before, are not clinical schizophrenics, but rather groups whose *characteristic movement* resists psychoanalysis fixated on the reductive "mommy-daddy-me" triangle. In *Anti-Oedipus,* the central "becoming" of schizophrenics, which resists the Oedipal resumption of the father's place, is "becoming-woman." Some feminists and others have taken Deleuze and Guattari to task for what they see as the sexism and even essentialism of this central concept. While the charge of sexism sometimes clings (Deleuze at least shows a remarkable tone-deafness to feminist concerns in texts such as his essay on masochism[19]), it would be hard to show, given the pair's philosophic context, that "becoming-woman" indulges essentialist tendencies. In any case, the concept features less centrally in the subsequent *A Thousand Plateaus*.

But more problematically, "becoming-woman" as the central process of becoming in *Anti-Oedipus* inadequately conveys the *group* nature of becoming. A group here means, of course, not a group *of individuals*, but a group more like a storm, a pack or a gang--defined by their movement in the same general direction, each "member" always only "partial."[20] D&G themselves are not two individuals, they say in the first lines of *A Thousand Plateaus*, but a sort of writing pack: "The two of us wrote *Anti-Oedipus* together. Since each of us was several, there was already quite a crowd." Such self-erasure, or "de-individualization," to use Foucault's word, aims to recover the insistent group formations of lives, taking a "line of flight" from the binaristic choice between individual agency and constructivism. The strategy aims "[t]o reach, not the point where one no longer says I, but the point where it is no longer of any importance whether one says I."[21]

"Becoming-woman" is then downplayed in *A Thousand Plateaus* for the new paradigmatic becoming of "becoming-animal," which remedies the overly personalized character of the former. Developing the concept of becoming-in-groups in several lengthy chapters, D&G first renarrate the story of Freud's famous patient the Wolf-Man, whose misdiagnosis after the dream of "five, six or seven wolves," they say, centered on the fact that neither Freud nor his successors knew what "[e]very child knows," that "wolves travel in packs" (ATP 28). Freud did not understand that the dream of the wolves was a dream of becoming-wolf:[22]

> It is not a question of representation: don't think for a minute that it has to do with believing oneself a wolf, representing oneself as wolf. The wolf, the wolves, are intensities, speeds, temperatures, nondecomposable variable distances. A swarming, a wolfing.

Later in the book D&G return us to the ongoing exploration of group becomings, generalizing the concept of becoming-wolf to the concept of becoming-animal. Becomings-animal happen around us all the time, but the dialectic modes of analysis most of us use are not adequate to recognize them. D&G warn again against collapsing becomings into a dialectic: "It is always possible to try to explain these blocks of becoming by a correspondence between two relations, but to do so most certainly impoverishes the phenomenon under study. ...A becoming is not a correspondence between relations ... neither is it a resemblance, an imitation, or, at the limit, an identification."[23] Becoming-animal will involve instead "endowing the parts of my body with relations of speed and slowness that will make it become-[animal], in an original assemblage proceeding neither by resemblance or analogy."[24] For example, in the "B" film *Willard* (1972, Daniel Mann), a young man becomes-rat[25]; in the Gospel of Matthew (5:9), the demon questioned by Jesus says, "My name is Legion," whereupon Jesus drives him into a herd of diving pigs[26]; in stories of witches, werewolves and vampires, people take on the movements of animals[27]; in lives of the Desert Fathers and other ascetics, we often find accounts of becomings-animal.[28]

c. The Nomads

After the exploration of becoming-animal, we finally arrive, in the "Treatise on Nomadology," at D&G's fullest exploration of the possibilities of becomings. The nomads, for D&G's purposes, are "humans" paradigmatic of becoming-animal. They "consist in being distibuted by turbulence across a smooth space, in producing movement that holds space and simultaneously affects all its points, instead of being held in space in local movement from one specified point to another."[29] This means, in concrete terms, that like the nomadic gypsies, Tuaregs or 15th-century Mongols, D&G's nomads remain oblivious to maps. Nomads conceptualize moving not as travel from point to point, but rather as a collective distribution across space at varying speeds at different times. Their object is simply to move, never to "get somewhere."

D&G designate by the term nomad any group that moves this way: "It is not the nomad who defines this constellation of characteristics; it is this constellation that defines the nomad."[30] For example, they say, bandits and gangs of all sorts,[31] some lobbyists,[32] ancient metallurgists and medieval alchemists,[33] religious heretics and soldiers in the holy wars of Christianity and Islam,[34] and even pieces in the Chinese game of Go[35] display the movement characteristic of nomads. In the present-day United States, it might be helpful to think of some truckdrivers, circus performers, residents of mobile homes, salespeople, migrant workers, and freelance construction workers as Deleuzoguattarian nomads as well.[36]

I have, as the reader will realize, spent a fair amount of time detailing D&G's theoretical intricacies; I would like now to turn at last to a reading of the text under consideration, *Paris is Burning*. For more than any of the examples so far suggested, the queens of *Paris is Burning* live to the fullest the characteristics of "becoming-nomad" described above.

4. The Nomadic Queens of *Paris is Burning*

It might strike us at first that D&G's rhapsodies on "becoming-woman" were tailor-made to fit the queens of *Paris is Burning*. Certainly the concept of "becoming-woman" pertains in fascinating ways. The queens are cross-dressers who, far from accepting an essentialist division between male/female, are constantly disrupting the notion that this duality exists at all. When speaking of themselves or others, the members of the families, or "children," never feel the need to determine, for themselves or the viewers, whether anyone is "really" a man or woman: they refer to the same person fluidly as "he" and "she." The implications of "becoming-woman" take current drag theory beyond its liberal moorings, in suggesting that drag is not best understood as identities assumed and shed, but as speeds and intensities of movement. The difference between drag theory ("you are what you wear") and D&G's "becoming-woman" ("you are how you move") is that the first re-entrenches the dialectical agent-action distinction, while the second implicates agent and action in each other.

The drag queens of *Paris is Burning* are even more promisingly considered, however, along the lines of D&G's second concept, "becoming-nomad." If the drag queen culture does not immediately strike us as a nomad group, nevertheless observing their "characteristic ways of moving" qualifies them as an instance of "becoming-nomad." While the point of understanding the drag queens as a collective becoming-nomad is not to "prove" D&G's theory, I hope to use their symptomatology to intersect and deflect other readings of the film that have focussed on the group's supposed victimization, oppression, false consciousness and escapism; to suggest the inadequacy of identity politics to account for certain aspects of their lives; and, to suggest the possibilities of a Deleuzoguattarian adialectic ethics to produce previously unimagined routes of action.

The first thing to keep in mind about the becomings D&G discuss is that they are not in any sense "imaginary" -- the imaginary being a category formed in response to the enforcement of only one "reality." The notion of a unitary reality, Deleuze and Guattari say in the "Treatise on Nomadology," belongs to objectivist, positivist conceptualizations of knowledge. D&G, doctrinaire social constructionists, instead believe in many different realities, dependent on perspective. The problem for them is not whether many realities exist, but rather, given state dissemination of the dogma of a unitary reality, how to remember or recognize these other realities when we see them. The science that recovers the multiplicity of realities from the obscurity of positivism is *nomadology*. Nomadology, D&G elaborate in this treatise, shatters the dialectic between state and individual and restores to sight the multitudinous "lines of flight," alternative realities, from those dialectic strictures.

a. To Be Real

The film *Paris is Burning* makes unitary reality a myth to be exploded from the first moments of the soundtrack, as the theme song, The Emotions' 1970s disco hit "To Be Real," plays in the background of the opening credits. "To Be Real" replays during the spectacular scene of the children walking the balls in the various categories, some dressed in the riding-gear of the English countryside, some in the nautical fashions of New England's upper crust, others in the street style of "banjee girls," and still others in the latest *haute couture* from Paris. The song takes on special significance as the camera cuts to Dorian Corey, *grande dame* and star of the movie. Dorian dispels in one breath the escapist and fantasy theories of the balls, intoning with ironic reverence that the balls are *real*: they are "not a take-off or a satire, no, it's actually being able to *be* this."

We are obviously in the presence of a real that most of us do not see. We are more comfortable conceding that the queens *want* to be real, or that the real of the real world is so harsh they must *imagine* a different real. But to understand the "real" that Dorian puts her finger on is an altogether different matter. In saying that the costumes, the mannerisms, the class aura, the body type, and the attitude of a particular ball-walker are "not a take-off or a satire, no, it's actually being able to *be* this," Dorian acknowledges the probable interpretation that the person is "merely" performing or satirizing, but in the same stroke insists that this misses the point. In short, in D&G's terms, the ballwalkers are not *representing*, they are *becoming*. We have stumbled upon a "line of flight."

b. Lines/Lives of Flight

But how do we know a "line of flight" when we see it? Well, we don't know anything, D&G respond, we simply declare it so; for "knowing" looks a lot different in nomadology than it does in royal science. Knowing nomadologically means resisting the impulse to crush complex multivalent forces into the dialectic format that royal science demands we use.

Still, if names can be applied to things according to their characteristic ways of moving, D&G find it important to flesh out the speeds and directions a becoming-nomad will follow, so that other instances can be named, celebrated and, most importantly, engaged. Some speeds and directions characteristic of nomadic ways of moving come to light in looking at (1) this gay subculture's strategic preying upon state institutions, (2) their unusual family formations, (3) the ethical investment in betrayal, (4) the violence of vogueing, and, finally, (5) their appropriation by state institutions.

(1) Attacking State Institutions

Flourishing in the midst of the city, the houses of the various families are far from wholly disengaged with the state institutions that surround them. They have to work, eat and pay rent more or less according to the rules. But the question need not be whether they are complicit with the state or subversive of it. The question could be, contrarily, whether relationality with the state figures centrally in their realities in the first place. The nomad group is indifferent to the state; their ways of moving have habituated them not to "understand" the dialectic relations the state enforces.[37] "It is true," D&G write, "that the nomads have no history; they only have a geography. ...Historians ... consider the nomads a pitiable segment of humanity that understands nothing."[38]

But this supposed lack of understanding, D&G say, might work in unexamined ways to ward off the formation of a state. For example, nomads in their various undertakings do not calculate with values like safety and longevity in mind. If nomad science designed a car, it would be a Yugo; if nomad science built a house, it would fall to pieces by the third winter. This does not mean that practitioners of nomadology are stupid; it means they do not value the values that enable state formation and ensure state continuity, such as longevity and safety. It is in this sense that D&G mean that nomad science "invents problems" and creates trouble for the state.[39] The state has to pick up the pieces after nomad encampments, figure out how to make nomad inventions (notably war!) sustainable and safe, and bureaucratize spaces where nomad wanderings have wreaked havoc.

For if the members of the various families seem to play along with the state rules, they are constantly launching subversive attacks on it as well. The balls are held around 5-7:00 *a.m.*, because, as one interviewee puts it, they are always "waiting for the working girls to get here." Many of the children work as prostitutes, a profession which makes trouble for state interest in controlling the mobility of labor. As D&G write, "one of the principal affairs of the State" has always undertaken to "conquer both a *band vagabondage* and *body nomadism*" by "[s]ettling [and] sedentarizing labor power, regulating the movement of the flow of labor, [and] assigning it channels and conduits."[40] The queens' vagabond families and wandering prostitutes unsettle the state's sedentarizing, measuring projects, such as taking censuses and collecting taxes.

Reinvesting the profits of prostitution in the drag world, the families create more trouble for the state by directing flows of capital away from state institutions and towards their own perpetuation: they buy fabric, sew, design outfits, arrange balls and spy on rivals. Even more troublesome, the families often divert capital they *haven't* earned:

Since one commonly "needs" a $4,000 evening dress by Yves St. Laurent to walk a ball, theft is institutionalized as the admired skill of "mopping." The queens "mop" not only expensive accessories and costumes but also daily amenities like food: The management of a certain Bronx fast-food place is mentioned for its egregious suckerdom.

(2) Nomad Families

The organization of the queens into Houses or families looks much more like the nomad pack than the state family; it is a "band vector," as D&G put it, "rather than a fundamental cell,"[41] or, it moves by "itineration" rather than "iteration and reiteration."[42] In terms more familiar to gay discourse, the drag queens families "reproduce" by recruitment rather than by sexual reproduction. And these families do recruit: The 11-year-old and 13-year-old interviewed on the street at 3 a.m. with their arms around each other are no longer sons of their mothers. "Ain't go no motha," one boy tells his questioner. "Ain't got no dad."

Whereas state families reproduce in multigenerational hereditary lines, the nomadic family pays little attention to hereditary lineage. The families in the drag queen culture could in no way be described as "healthy" families in state terminology. All members of all the families are on the lam from their genetic parents, which in itself is enough to constitute them as refugees from the state. Neither does the continuation of a family happen in the usual oedipal way; rather, a family forms when a ballwalker has accumulated enough trophies and prizes to be considered a "legend." She then starts accepting protégés, her "children," and she becomes the "mother" of the new House. The House depends entirely on the charisma and lifespan of the mother, not on any system of inheritance; the best protégé does not automatically take over the parentage of the house when the mother falls out of favor or dies. The preeminence of a House at any one moment depends not on inheritance, but on flows and breakdowns of power.

And power does break down. The nomad groups suffer casualties in their stance towards the state: one of the prize children of the House of Xtravaganza, Venus Xtravaganza, is strangled by a trick in the course of filming. While she is missed, her death does not affect the families in easily predictable ways. Her death is mentioned as part of the "struggle," conceptualized more as a casualty of war than a death in the family. In a nomadic conceptualization, Venus as warrior "is caught up in a series of exploits leading him to solitude and a prestigious but powerless death."[43] Individuals are not missed in a pack in the same way they are missed in a family.

These flows and breakdowns of power may misserve a particular "individual" or family at a particular time, but they actually ensure the survival of the nomad pack as a whole. As D&G describe it, "a genealogy is transferred from one family to another according to the aptitude of a given family at a given time to realize the maximum of ... solidarity"[44] (ATP 366). When Venus Xtravaganza is murdered, the symbolic capital she held for her House is transferred or entrusted to the glory of another House, in the form of group recognition of another "upcoming legend," for the mutual survival of all the families.

It sounds insensitive. It sounds amoral. And so it is, from the traditional "family values" viewpoint of liberal democracy. But it must be clear at this point that we are dealing with a set of family values we hardly recognize.

(3) Throwing Shade

The *Paris is Burning* nomads cause trouble for state institutions in other ways, as well. In state discourses, virtues such as honor, truthfulness and loyalty are held in high esteem, while their opposite vices are penalized. In nomad land, alternatively, the so-called virtues and vices have no referent except a particular practitioner in a particular context. For this reason, the queen cultures can accommodate and even institutionalize backbiting, insulting and betrayal. All such behavior, D&G maintain, "animate[s] a fundamental indiscipline of the warrior, a questioning of hierarchy, perpetual blackmail by abandonment or betrayal, and a very volatile sense of honor, all of which, once again, impedes the formation of the State."[45]

The reason for the nomads' unusual moral negotiations amounts to a matter of survival in the face of "turbulence" or violence.[46] While violence will always exceed the dialectic structures of the state, causing it to externalize violence in the form of convenient enemies against whom the state must wage war, the nomad group institutionalizes structures of "sustainable" violence that obviate the creation of external enemies. These structures "institute an entire economy of violence, in other words, mak[e] violence durable, even unlimited"[47] (ATP 396). This is why the nomadic family--a moving battle, a battle in motion--is not the same as an army, which stands or falls with its last battle.[48] The nomad group, sustaining violence within its own structures, thrives on a dynamic of constant decomposing and regrouping. Winning a grand battle, the ultimate expression of the state dialectic, will not get one very far in the world of the balls.

(4) Vogueing and Violence

On the other hand, sustained violence--what we might commonly call dirty play--will get one quite far. While state violence annihilates, nomad violence sustains. In the drag queen underground, violence is institutionalized at a number of levels and has a number of names. The first level at which a queen challenges a rival is called the "read," performed by finding some flaw in the rival's appearance and exaggerating it. When you get a laugh, Dorian says, "then you have a good read going." The second level is "throwing shade"--and I note with interest that D&G write, "[a]nything that throws or is thrown is fundamentally a weapon."[49] Dorian explains throwing shade as the art of apprising the rival of his flaws by the minutest insults or gestures, with the effect of saying, "You're ugly, but I don't have to tell you you're ugly, because you know you're ugly." At this stage, Dorian says, all sense of honour goes out the window; "you're getting 'em any way you can. ...The children will stop at nothing." The characteristic dance form of black gay male culture, vogueing, arose as further refinement of throwing shade: Two antagonists duel in their moves around each other on the dance floor, the "winner" being the voguer who can maneuver as intricate a meshing with the other voguer's dancing body without actually touching him. This is not violence as a conventional "fight"; it is violence as a way of moving.

Vogueing as the highest version of institutionalized sustained violence in the drag queen culture may seem to be self-contained and therefore "ineffective," until we realize that a state cannot form in spaces where violence is part of the flows and fluxes of reality, rather than a coagulated and externalized separate entity. The costume balls as wars between families ward off state structures. "It's taken very seriously," Dorian says. "They say they're just fun but believe me they're wars." In fact, sustained wars, D&G write, are "the surest mechanism directed against the formation of the State." They continue, "War maintains the dispersal and segmentarity of groups ... just as Hobbes saw clearly that *the State was against war, so war is against the State."* Against the grain of our liberal democratic tendencies, D&G suggest, we might want to consider that societies which have not "yet," in social Darwinist terms, "developed" into state organizations, are precisely and wisely "wandering" away from that form. "[T]he implication is that primitive people 'don't understand' so complex an apparatus. ...[Instead] it is ... a potential concern of primitive societies to ward off that monster they supposedly do not understand," they write.[50]

(5) Appropriation

That the institutionalized violence of the drag queen subculture wards off state formations does not mean, however, that they are wholly immunized against state appropriation. In fact, D&G say that it is ironically only state formation that can provide structures to immunize groups against appropriation. Such immunities, for example, might take the form of identities. The granting of coherent, stable, unassailable identities is, after all, a state specialty. But nomad group formations provide no such innoculating measures. While nomadology can certainly "invent problems," only the state can solve them.[51] D&G are not concerned that nomad groups and states seem to interact all the time, for such interaction seems only to provide more fuel for the enterprises of the nomads: "The necessity of maintaining the most rigorous of distinctions between sedentaries, migrants and nomads does not preclude *de facto* mixes."[52] But if the nomads constantly mingle, they never gain the upper hand, and D&G know it. The nomadic social structures in fact insure that they won't. Without the discipline and values of state structures, nomads are wholly susceptible to the incursions and appropriations of an imperialist state. For example, if the the queens at moments successfully prey upon the fashion and advertising industries--both rackets which are intensively complicitous in reproducing state desires, as many critics of *Paris is Burning* have pointed out--they equally often yearn for its comforts, aspiring to jobs, fame and domestic bliss in the "normal world."[53] Some of the queens' statements seem downright regressive: "To be able to blend--that's what realness is ... to pass to the trained or untrained eye" and not reveal you're gay; "that's when it's real," says one interviewee. Another admits that the whole drag queen underground could be seen as "a case of going back into the closet."

But reading the costume balls as an extended exercise in the strategies of "passing" would require eliding the subtleties of what the queens seem to mean by "realness," of their indifference to state institutions, of the family structures, of the practices of sustainable violence that keep state formations at bay. This is a culture in which no prize is awarded for passing. Honor here is due to *becomings* of all sorts: becoming-sailor, becoming business-man, becoming-woman, becoming-schoolboy. The children do not fall out of "character," or at least less and less so as their becomings progress with each passing ball. They are permanently transubstantiated. Octavia Saint Laurent, mother of the House of Saint Laurent, has become-woman thoroughly enough to cut up the opposite sex in true sister style: "I think all men are dogs," she laments with no trace of irony. "I really do. They all start barking sooner or later."

5. Conclusion: Illiberal Ethics as Faith

At last I come to the end of this adventure, having challenged the ascendancy of identity politics with a reading of *Paris is Burning* through Deleuze and Guattari's nomadology. At the end of this reading, I am left excited by the ethical possibilities for groups to desire and produce in only idiosyncratic relationship to the state--in other words, by the possibilities of more sorts of action to "count" as "ethical" action. I am also disturbed by the objections that could be raised against such a reading. In a word, with the queens talking about "passing" and "going back into the closet," becoming-nomad does not necessarily seem to advance gay rights in the liberal sense. After all, isn't it the case that state appropriation is the partial fate of nomad groups?

One could look at the glass half-empty or half-full. Half-empty, states always appropriate nomad groups. Half-full, states can never appropriate nomad groups entirely. That is why identity politics, in its dialectic with the state, proves inadequate to describing the queens documented in *Paris is Burning*, Articles lamenting the "disintegration" and "collapse" of the drag world, such as the *New York Times* two-day series on the occasion of Angie Xtravaganza's death, must be interrogated further: What do words like "disintegration" and "collapse" mean, if nomad groups work by breaking down?[54] Articles noting the film's pre-AIDS-conscious "poignancy," such as the same paper's 1991 review, should be challenged: Can we invent other, non-victimizing conceptualizations of the disease?[55]

If the AIDS crisis has been the litmus test for contemporary gay ethics, perhaps I should conclude by surmising what a Deleuzoguattarian reading of the ethics of *Paris is Burning* could contribute to ways of coming to terms with AIDS. Yet such a coming to terms will incorporate the same sort of sustainable violence that coheres the *Paris is Burning* group, and the same violence from which most sympathetic discussants of AIDS recoil. Deleuze, who considers his philosophical project as a "kind of ass-fuck,"[56] and Guattari, a lifelong activist for gay liberation, wrote *A Thousand Plateaus* in 1980, just before AIDS became imperative to address. But this need not mean their gay-relevant writings are reductively naive or "poignant." At moments their discussion of epidemic in *A Thousand Plateaus* eerily predicts a disease like AIDS that reproduces by contagion rather than heredity. But their thoughts of such an epidemic, which mirrors the state-impeding characteristics of nomadic groups, carry an unmistakable celebratory tone:[57]

> How can we conceive of a peopling, a propagation, a becoming that is without filiation or hereditary production? A multiplicity without the unity of an ancestor? It is quite simple; everybody knows it, but it is discussed only in secret. We oppose epidemic to affiliation, contagion to heredity, peopling by contagion to sexual reproduction. ...Bands, human or animal, proliferate by contagion, epidemics, battlefields, and catastrophes.

The contrast of straight reproduction to gay proliferation is nothing new; from stories of "the recruit" to themes of vampirism, gay narratives abound with instances of unusual proliferative methods. But in the context of AIDS, D&G's talk of "peopling by contagion" could sound, at best, romantic and, at worst, reckless.

Then again, I am reminded that Foucault called D&G's *Anti-Oedipus* "a book of ethics." Known for his belief that AIDS, like everything else, is a "product of power," Foucault too has been accused variously of naiveté, poignancy, romanticism and recklessness in his conceptualizations of the disease. Is there some sense in which we might understand Foucault to have revalued romantic-to-reckless conceptualizations as more "ethically" satisfying? Did Deleuze and Guattari's recovery of groups without identity--that is, groups unidentifiable in terms of state recognition--contribute to Foucault's peculiar "line of flight" from the binary HIV victim/aggressor labels available in liberal democratic usage? Could he have found AIDS activism to gain in ethical stature the more it shook itself free of responsiveness to the state?

I find that as scholars of religion, we have at our disposal a vocabulary particularly tailored to handle concepts otherwise labeled romantic or reckless: It is the vocabulary of faith. Knowing nomadologically, instead of positively, declaratively instead of rationally, turns out to look a lot like what we often call faith. Might D&G's announcement of the proliferation of nomadic groups profitably be considered as a confession of faith? Could the *Paris is Burning* queens, whirling and whoring on the outside of state structures, be more richly conceived as believers than as deluded freaks?

I would not be the first to suggest that the gay movement could to advantage liken itself to a faith of sorts. Two writers in gay film theory have also turned to "belief" or "faith" as a new context for theorizing. Richard Dyer, author of a study in gay and lesbian film, suggests in a famous article that certain facets of gay politics finally cannot be negotiated except by "believing in fairies."[58] Film theorist Jane Gaines admits also that belief in gay presence "always requires an act of faith that is politically problematic in other ways."[59] In his *Village Voice* article "Faith, Hope and Sodomy," Richard Goldstein draws on the gay motif of alternative proliferation to suggest the gay movement's potential resources in religious discourse--religion being another famous arena of recruitment. "[I]f we framed gayness as a faith," Goldstein writes, "we might finally stop asking impossible questions, such as: Is it chosen or is it innate? We accept the paradoxical nature of religious beliefs. They are both chosen and essential."

Unfortunately Goldstein takes this fascinating proposal to see gayness as a faith in a conventional liberal direction. "If we understood [gayness] as an awakening comparable to religious revelation, we might be better able to make a space for it in society," he writes. "[T]here is [a] distinctly American possibility: that gayness, taken as a faith, will find a place for itself in the landscape of revelation, no more threatening than Jehovah's Witnesses and a lot less likely to ring your doorbell."[60] On the other hand, D&G allow a conceptualization of religion as a potentially revolutionary force, as long as it remains unlocatable in the liberal democratic landscape of which Goldstein speaks: "We are referring to religion as an element in a [nomad group] and the idea of holy war as the motor" of that group.[61] The faith approach to gay politics, or ethics, allows a new viewpoint on the *Paris is Burning* drag queens. Their gay lives, insistently incommensurable with available liberal identities, could start to make sense as lives of faith.

---

[1] Livingston, Jennie. *Paris is Burning*, videocassette (Academy Entertainment, 1992).

[2] Throughout this paper I will use "gay" to refer to those who consider themselves gay men, or who, at least, do not consider them-

selves lesbians or straights. If it is certainly problematic to isolate the term "gay" with one sex, I judge it would be more problematic to either refer to the two very different gay and lesbian cultures as one, or to try to do justice to both in one paper.

[3] Jesse Green, "Paris has Burned," *New York Times* (18 April 1993).

[4] I often use the "state" as shorthand for a government and its institutions. In adopting French thinkers Deleuze and Guattari's terminology of the "state" here (they capitalize "State"), I mean, as I think they do, to refer to the majoritarian social formations in some particular place and time, not some Marxist monolith. In the case of the the black drag queen culture of New York City, I take the state to be the institutions and compulsions of liberal democracy.

[5] Gilles Deleuze and Félix Guattari, *Anti-Oedipus: Capitalism and Schizophrenia* (Minneapolis: University of Minnesota Press, 1983); *A Thousand Plateaus: Capitalism and Schizophrenia* (Minneapolis: University of Minnesota Press, 1987).

[6] Deleuze and Guattari, *Anti-Oedipus*, pp. 4-8.

[7] D&G, *A Thousand Plateaus*, p. 422.

[8] This treatise constitutes Chapter 12 of Deleuze and Guattari, *A Thousand Plateaus*, pp. 351-423; its full title is "1227: Treatise on Nomadology--The War Machine."

[9] Don DeLillo, *White Noise* (New York: Penguin, 1984).

[10] Richard Goldstein, "Faith, Hope and Sodomy," *Village Voice* (29 June 1993), pp. 21-23+.

[11] Deleuze and Guattari, *A Thousand Plateaus*, p. 372.

[12] Goldstein, p. 22.

[13] Michel Foucault, *Power/Knowledge: Selected Interviews and Other Writings, 1972-1977* (New York: Pantheon, 1980), p. 136.

[14] Denise Riley, *Am I That Name? Feminism and the Category of 'Women' in History* (Minneapolis: University of Minnesota Press, 1988), p. 96.

[15] Michel Foucault, *Discipline and Punish* (New York: Vintage, 1979).

[16] Gilles Deleuze, *Foucault* (Minneapolis: University of Minnesota Press, 1988).

[17] Foucault , *Power/Knowledge*, p. 80.

[18] Foucault, Introduction, in Deleuze and Guattari, *Anti-Oedipus*, pp. xiii-xiv.

[19] Gilles Deleuze, "Coldness and Cruelty," *Masochism* (New York: Zone Books, 1991), pp. 9-138.

[20] D&G understand "partial objects" to be a greatly undertheorized concept which psychoanalysis uncovered and then abandoned in terror (*Anti-Oedipus*, pp. 42-43). The relationship of the part to the whole figures centrally throughout D&G's work together, and in Deleuze's philosophic texts. As Deleuze explains in *Cinema 1: The Movement-Image* (Minneapolis: University of Minnesota Press, 1986), the whole "is not a set and does not have parts. It is rather that which prevents each set, however big it is, from closing in on itself" (p. 16).

[21] Deleuze and Guattari, *A Thousand Plateaus*, p. 3.

[22] *Ibid.*, p. 32.

[23] *Ibid.*, p. 237.

[24] *Ibid.*, p. 258.

[25] *Ibid.*, p. 233.

[26] *Ibid.*, p. 239.

[27] *Ibid.*, p. 241.

[28] *Ibid.*, p. 247.

[29] *Ibid.*, p. 363.

[30] *Ibid.*, p. 422.

[31] *Ibid.*, p. 358

[32] *Ibid.*, p. 366.

[33] *Ibid.*, p. 372.

[34] *Ibid.*, p. 383.

[35] *Ibid.*, p. 353.

[36] D&G go on to say that this same habitual movement of nomads by distribution at different speeds across a space constitutes "war machines," entities mentioned in the subtitle of the "Treatise on Nomadology: The War Machine." For my purposes in this paper, I will consider nomad groups and war machines to be synonymous.

[37] Deleuze and Guattari, *A Thousand Plateaus*, p. 354.

[38] *Ibid.*, p. 393.

[39] *Ibid.*, p. 374.

[40] *Ibid.*, p. 368.

[41] *Ibid.*, p. 366.

[42] *Ibid.*, p. 372.

[43] *Ibid.*, p. 357.

[44] *Ibid.*, p. 366.

[45] *Ibid.*, p. 358.

[46] *Ibid.*, p. 363.
[47] *Ibid.*, p. 396.
[48] *Ibid.*, p. 418-420.
[49] *Ibid.*, p. 395.
[50] *Ibid.*, p. 357.
[51] *Ibid.*, p. 374.
[52] *Ibid.*, p. 384.

[53] Since this film was made, a number of articles have noted the longstanding and increasing appropriation of the drag queen world by the fashion industry: for example, Willi Ninja, Mother of the House of Ninja, went on from this film to become the world's most famous voguer and bring vogueing to high-fashion runways (Green, "Paris has Burned," p. 11).

[54] Green, "Paris has Burned," and Jesse Green, "Film, Fame, Fade-out: The Drag World in Collapse," *New York Times* (19 April 1993).

[55] Jennifer Dunning, "Exotic Gay Subculture Turns Poignant," *New York Times* (23 March 1991).

[56] *Ibid.*, p. x.
[57] *Ibid.*, p. 241.

[58] Richard Dyer, "Believing in Fairies: The Author and the Homosexual," in Diana Fuss (ed.), *Inside/Out: Lesbian Theories, Gay Theories* (London: Routledge, 1991), pp. 185-201. Also see his book, *Now You See It: Studies on Gay and Lesbian Film* (London: Routledge, 1990).

[59] Jane Gaines, "Dorothy Arzner's Trousers," *Jump Cut*, no. 37 (Spring 1992), p. 90.

[60] Richard Goldstein, *The Village Voice* (X XX x) p. 29.

[61] Deleuze and Guattari, *A Thousand Plateaus*, p. 383.

J. Michael Clark

Erotic Empowerment, Ecology, & Eschatology,
or, Sex, Earth, & Death in the Age of AIDS

---

1. An Erotic Ecology

Because my theology has progressively interwoven feminist thought and sexual, gay male experience, I have realized that our sexuality at its best is not only an urging into relationship with another person, but also an urging for justice in all relationships, including our relationship with the earth itself.[1] Following Jim Nelson, for example, I have suggested that our sexuality is a complex nexus of emotional, psychological, and spiritual, as well as bodily experiences: making love to ourselves, befriending one another, expressing our love for our special beloveds, and moving us both to encounter the divine and to seek justice not only in the bedroom but throughout our lives. The erotic, or more concretely in our experience, our sexuality, becomes a meaningless, genitally reduced notion *unless* we understand the erotic as part and parcel of our urges toward mutuality and human(e)ness. Our fundamental need for connectedness, love, and self-affirming acceptance--our erotic and sexual drive toward connectedness with all things--undergirds our quest for mutuality and, through the realization of that quest, empowers our efforts to establish justice in *all* relationships, not just our sexually expressed ones. In other words, our sexuality is not so much about where and how we put our genitals, but is rather something that permeates our lives and that both urges us toward and sustains our relationships--even those that are not genitally consummated ones. As the power of relation, our sexuality enables--nay, compels--liberational, justice-seeking activity in the world. Nelson reiterates this idea when he says that the divine eros is "that fundamental energy of the universe that is the passion for connection and hence the hunger for justice and yearning for life-giving communion."[2]

This erotic oneness also shapes our deepest valuing and acting in the world. While Nelson merely suggested in an earlier book that "compassion ... is intimately related to our sexuality," more recently he has forthrightly argued that our embodiment as sexual beings is in fact foundational to our capacities to feel (and to enact) compassion.[3] Our sexual embodiment is actually *necessary* for us to be moral creatures. He says, for example, "Moral knowledge ... is bodily: if we cannot somehow feel in the gut the meanings of justice and injustice, of hope and hopelessness, those terms remain abstract and unreal."[4] I would argue, therefore, that our embodied capacity for compassion and our embodied capacity for justice-making are one and the same; compassion in action, which *is* justice-seeking and -making, is borne in and from our erotically or sexually informed drive toward right-relation. I would also argue that the love-making and justice-making (the right-relationship-making) that I begin at home with my spouse should permeate and inform all my relationships and value concerns. In fact, the care and tenderness of our specific relationships *must* inform all our values, all our ways of relating to and seeking justice within the world, lest we remain in conflict with ourselves: One cannot make-love and make-hate simultaneously.

So, if we are not alienated from our genital activity, but have instead fully and holistically realized the healing and shaping power of the erotic--of our sexuality--as something that permeates, shapes, and even creates our drive toward and our energies for sustaining our most intimate relationship(s), how can we *not* experience that energy carried over, carried out of, our committed sexual relationships in such a fashion that it influences all our value-laden interactions with the world, in terms of *both* our human and nonhuman fellow creatures? As my understanding of erotic empowerment has expanded to encompass that energy which not only compels justice-making in all my human relationships, but which also compels justice-making in all other relationships as well, including my relationship to the "earth and all that dwell therein," I am led to share Anne Primavesi's contention that "sexuality sensitizes the entire body to respond to all other forms of life in the world--person, animal, flower, or river."[5] Moreover, if the erotic, or concretely our sexuality, leads us to affirm that erotic empowerment also informs ecology, then we have to address our specific sexuality as well. In other words, we have to inquire as to what the specific experiences and perspectives of being gay in a homophobic society (and a society also permeated by AIDS) can bring to ecological discourse.[6]

Ultimately, neither gay men and lesbians, nor women, nor people of color, nor native Americans, nor any other oppressed people can afford to wait for a white, heteromale conferral of authority to speak--neither in politics, nor in theology, nor in ecology. The earth, our home in the broadest possible sense, cannot afford to wait for the status quo's championing either. We must assume and assert our own *a priori* prophetic authoritativeness to "speak from

God's point of view."[7] Our authority to speak is actually borne out of our experience of oppression: Our exclusion as gay men and lesbians in a heterosexist and homophobic ethos stands in judgment upon both canon and tradition and explodes their boundaried exclusivity. Moreover, the solidarity of oppression means that as we assert and create our own liberation from exclusion and objectification (our disvaluation as merely sexual and hence subhuman beings), so also are we obliged to seek the liberation of other persons, and of the very earth itself, from objectification, devaluation and disvaluation, and exploitation.

This critical stance suggests that gay and lesbian experience and theology can in fact contribute something unique to ecological reflection and analysis. With great irony we realize that the process of legally extending rights democratically first to African Americans, then to women, and, to some as yet all too limited extent to endangered species and the environment, is nothing but a so called liberal progression which has conveniently passed over certain groups which are still deemed invisible at best and aesthetically or morally undesirable at worst and which, therefore, remain disenfranchised--most native Americans, the poor and the homeless, and gay men and lesbians. These groups of people and all too much of the biosphere as well are, if not invisible even in liberal analyses, treated as devalued, disvalued, and disposable. Disvaluation and disposability not only affect our gay and lesbian lives through anti-gay/lesbian violence and AIDS-apathy, but also continue to shape environmental attitudes as well. As a result, our voices must continue to be raised against any cultural narrow-mindedness which sanctions anti-gay/lesbian violence, which sanctions apathetic and even judgmentally punitive attitudes toward AIDS among gay men, IV-drug users, the poor, and third world peoples of color, and which also sanctions the exploitation and disposability of the earth.

In fact, we may wish to construct our gay liberation ecotheological analysis in contradistinction to that of primarily male "deep ecology" and as a further extension of that of ecofeminism. According to deep ecology, an *anthropo*centric world view of human self-centeredness or selfishness has led to environmental problems; in contrast, according to ecofeminism, an *andro*centric world view of masculine privilege and social structures has devalued and exploited both women and nature.[8] Gay ecotheology will insist that both these views are incomplete; the predominantly western, white, heteromasculinist world view is the problem. Not only are women, nature, and sexuality *de*-valued, but heteropatriarchy's hierarchy of values and categories *dis*values diversity. Reductionism exploits and destroys anyone and anything designated as "other." What we see is not just a *de*valuing which leads to domination and exploitation, but a *dis*valuing which strips away all value and which thereby leads to exclusion, to being disposable, to being acceptable for extinction.

This then becomes the basis for the uniqueness of our gay voice, in collaborative and creative extension of feminist analysis. Gay liberation theology has elsewhere noted that while feminist theology adequately deals with issues of human evil and responsibility for oppression, in view of AIDS gay theology must also wrestle with natural evil and theodicy and thereby synthesize a theology which addresses both human evil (homophobia) and natural evil (AIDS).[9] Likewise in the ecological arena, gay ecotheology must move beyond the issues of domination and exploitation to those of disvaluation, exclusion, and expendability in order to synthesize a theology which radically celebrates diversity and the equal and intrinsic value of all that is, whether the human, the biospheric, or the geospheric. Ecofeminism has articulately addressed the patriarchal hierarchy of value which *de*values (which lowers value) in order to dominate, use, and exploit. Gender roles and sexist exploitation are paradigmatic illustrations. Gay ecotheology must extend this to address the *hetero*patriarchal hierarchy of value which *dis*values (which strips of all value) in order to get rid of, to use up, to dispose of as having no further use or no use whatsoever. Exclusion, expendability, and the denial of the value of diversity are paradigmatic illustrations. While ecofeminists work over against the devaluation and domination of self and world as utilitarian objects for a masculine society, gay ecotheology must work over against the disvaluation and exclusion of self and world as disposable, worthless commodities in a heterosexist society which disdains diversity and eliminates the unnecessary--that which has no utilitarian value.

Ecofeminist Anne Primavesi has noted that "by becoming aware of patterns of domination [and exploitation] in our own lives, we learn to connect these patterns with the domination of nonhuman nature."[10] Indeed we do, for we are reminded that the same dualisms which link nature, women, and sexuality extend to gay and lesbian people who are also viewed as primarily and excessively sexual and unspiritual. We, too, are subject to heteropatriarchy's devaluing and disvaluing reductionism. In fact, our experience of total disvaluation as value*less* (or even as "bad") and of violence against us as gay men and lesbians enables us also to see the extent to which our society also disvalues nature and acts violently upon both the human and nonhuman environment. For us, disvaluation, exclusion, and disposability must also factor into ecological analysis, in addition to devaluation, exploitation, and domination, because we see our society virtually willing to throw away our earth, our home, as well as because we carry within our collective memory an awareness of just how often human beings themselves have been treated as expendable and disposable.

In the history of the gay and lesbian communities, never has our own expendability been so evident as in the rising incidence of anti-gay/lesbian violence and particularly in the AIDS health crisis. The same value hierarchy that insists that nature is reducible to expendable resources also insists on dichotomizing innocent and not innocent (read: expendable) victims of AIDS. Our government has spent money in the pursuit of testing protocols and vaccines, while our politico-medical system has resisted approving treatment protocols and finding a cure. Gay men, IV-drug users, people of color, and third world countries where AIDS rages *heterosexually* are still devalued and/or disvalued. Our expendability mitigates the urgency of cure or treatment. We are being treated as expendable objects to be used up or found useless and then discarded. And the experience of our expendability becomes a paradigmatic metaphor for western culture's attitudes toward all the earth. Hence, our gay ecotheology must adamantly oppose *any* disvaluation and exclusion which leads to dispensing with diversity and disposing of life. Neither gay men and lesbians, nor the biosphere, nor the geosphere, nor any of the great diversity which god/ess creates and delights in is expendable.

As we (re)confront heteropatriarchal abuses and theological categories which imperil the environment, we can begin to create a gay ecotheology which discloses that our gay and lesbian existence is not only a mode of being-*in*-the-world, but also a way of being-*with*-the-world as copartners in the inclusive processes of healing and liberation and thereby in the quest for and realization of justice as right-relation *throughout the earth*. As we experience our consciousness changing--as we realize the absolutely equal and intrinsic value of all that is, as well as the fundamental and erotically informed interconnectedness, relationality, and interdependence of all things within the web of Being--we cannot help but question the human arrogance which has permeated heteropatriarchy. We are in fact compelled to exchange egocentrism for ecocentrism, to exchange anthropocentrism for what Anne Primavesi has termed "ecological humility."[11] "Ecological humility" can also be understood as part and parcel of an important Jewish concept. The concept of *tikkun olam* entails our obligation to be about the business of repairing the world, both in its human and non-human, its biospheric and geospheric aspects. It does not assume that humanity is the pinnacle of creation, but rather celebrates the intrinsic value and rich diversity of all that is and reminds us of our humble interdependence within the web of being. *Tikkun olam* therefore also requires that we assume the tasks of caring, cooperation, *and* responsibility and of justice as right-relation throughout the earth. It is our obligation to love the earth and to love life itself, even though we are mortal and our individual lives must end.[12]

2. An Ecology of Dying

Because I am both gay and HIV+, it is precisely the confluence of mortality and *tikkun olam* which has become a pressing concern for me. And, that specific concern brings me to the topic of "eschatology," a term which certainly requires some deconstructing and reconstructing. What I am specifically interested in exploring is what an erotically empowered, ecological theology has to say about death: How do I resolve the very personal confluence of sex and death in my own community and in my own life, if I am to do so informed by my ecological reflections?

Studying ecological theory and beginning to have one's own theology and praxis reconstructed by ecologically sound values discloses one thing with increasing vividness: Our traditional Christian understandings of eschatology--of death as somehow not-death, not really--have had extremely negative environmental consequences. Traditional eschatology has functioned as yet one more sanction for devaluing and, ultimately, disvaluing the earth and this embodied life. As Catherine Keller has noted, the "drive to transcendent unity" with the divine, outside or beyond this life and this world, is "a profound impetus in all patriarchal spirituality, and it always achieves its end at the expense of nature and multiplicity."[13] Devaluing this earth inevitably leads to the careless disvaluing of the diversity of life on earth by means of exploitation to the point of the extinction of species; eliminating complexity works toward eliminating *any* viable future for life on earth. The real danger beneath transcendent, eschatological spirituality becomes frighteningly clear: Patriarchal, linear thinking assumes both a literal beginning ("creation") and a literal ending ("eschaton"). Coupled with a transcendent, otherworldly spirituality, such linear thinking also implies that we can or that we should work the earth toward that end and thereby hasten the arrival of the "next" world. Such otherworldliness not only devalues and disvalues this world, but actually sanctions exhausting a clearly expendable earth.

The logical alternative to otherworldly eschatology, however, is very difficult to accept. Watching so many of our friends die "due to complications from AIDS" before their fortieth birthdays, while we monitor our own health and bodies and T-cell counts, altogether makes the idea that when we die, we're dead. Period. End of subject(ivity). ...altogether extremely unpalatable. And yet, other ecological writers will not allow us to pursue escapist solutions to this dilemma. Karl Peters, for example, named our shared dilemma in his 1992 American Academy of Religion roundtable paper when he said, "The atomistic, individualistic understanding of human nature makes it very difficult to see that there is anything positive for ourselves in our own dying."[14] And, he's right. An isolated and individualistic understanding of human nature is so ingrained in us that we obsess about the loss in death of our individual, subjective, experiencing center--what Peters calls the "phenomenal self"[15]--and we will do anything in our mental, spiritual, and physical power to avoid confronting our own mortality and dealing with our own death as THE END. Peters argues that we *must* instead come to see ourselves "in a bigger picture, not just as individuals but as part of larger systems," as part of familial and relational networks, as interwoven within the biosphere, the geosphere, and the cosmos.[16] In her most recent book, Rosemary Radford Ruether also challenges this stubborn individualism which clings to the phenomenal self, because this individualism both denies death and disvalues (other) life.[17] Our "personal selves" or "phenomenal selves" are transient. Just as we emerged out of a greater oneness, through conception and birth (out of erotic empowerment if you will), and have "individuated" throughout our embodied lives, so in death we must relinquish individuality and merge back into oneness.

While this is very hard for our phenomenal, subjective selves to accept, an ecological perspective may help mitigate our dilemma. Ruether reminds us, for example, that "in nature, death is not an enemy, but a friend of the life process. The death side of the life cycle is an essential component of that renewal of life by which dead organisms are broken down and become the nutrients of new organic growth."[18] Peters echoes her wisdom when he similarly says, "In a finite world, the possibilities of existence can only be actualized in sequences in which some things give way to other things. ...Death is a necessary good in that it allows for new forms of life, new ways of living and thinking to be born."[19] He even goes so far as to argue that it may be possible to see our individual deaths "as contributing to the good of both others and ourselves in the context of ongoing human society and continuing [non-human] life on our planet."[20] If the ecological wisdom of Ruether and Peters still seems to fly in the face of our inherited and deeply internalized, western Christian eschatological denial of personal death, perhaps to get beyond Christianity we must first get behind it.

Our earlier Judaic roots do not encourage either individualism or death-denial. Two key elements (among others) for a Judaic ecology are relationality (with god/ess and the world, intimately and covenantally interwoven one with the other) and mortality (as human limitation and as limits on human power, use, and abuse). In fact, prior to Hellenic influences, Judaism "saw mortality as natural rather than a problem to be overcome. Its vision of blessedness had focused on a healthy and prosperous life in a full term of years, not escape from mortality altogether."[21] Just as the mandate of *tikkun olam* precluded an exploitative relationship to the earth, so an ecology built upon the cyclical renewal of earth and creatures, most notably in the periodic Jubilee year, precluded linear, apocalyptic, end-time thinking prior to the rise of later messianic expectation. According to Ruether, this Jewish perspective that "mortality is our natural condition, which we share with all other earth beings, and that redemption is the fullness of life within these limits, is a more authentic ethic for ecological living,"[22] and, I would add, ecological dying as well.

...All of which brings me back to Karl Peters' roundtable paper. He basically defines the phenomenal self as a "symbiotic union of biology and culture."[23] This "symbiotic union" is clearly relational and interactive, because he goes on to say that, "as webs of reality, each of us has the possibility of continuing in particular ways beyond the death of our phenomenal selves"; moreover, "our cultural, biological, and cosmic continuation constitute a kind of immortality, *not of ourselves as self-conscious subjects*, but a kind of objective immortality--of how we continue in terms of our influences on others in our society, on the human life form, on other forms of life, and even on the earth itself."[24] Peters implicitly shares an important ethical and ecological mandate with the early Jewish perspective: We are called to construct our lives so as to make positive, quality of life differences in the lives of others, both human and nonhuman, both biospheric and geospheric alike. "Objective immortality" then means that our impact on the quality of life for others and for the earth itself continues; even without ego, or names, or other individualistic identification--and certainly without individual, subjective, phenomenal experience--our influence is interwoven into the ongoing, processive cycles of the web of being. The question remains, however, as to whether even "objective" immortality, just by the very use of the word "immortality," doesn't risk becoming just one more ruse by which we avoid confronting the very hard reality of our own personal death. That when we die, it's over. Ended. Period. And this is where I get stuck.

Both intellectually and ecologically I know that life and death are one, that just as we came out of that oneness, we must return to it. Any otherworldly eschatology is certainly ecologically untenable. Any immortality beyond that of our attention to and impact upon the quality of life for others and for the earth itself, here and now, is impossible and, ultimately, undesirable. I cannot fathom what it would be like to live forever, nor do I think I would really want to. At the same time, I definitely don't want life to be over any time soon. I certainly don't want my subjective experience of my relational network to come to an end. Specifically, I do not want to leave my spouse and our home and constructed family behind, and I do not want him to leave me behind, either. I do not want *anyone else* to leave "due to complications from AIDS." And yet, I cannot deny the reality and the finality of death for my phenomenal self, for my subjective, experiencing, individual self. I am left not with some calmly, objectively achieved, intellectual truth, but rather with the paradox of two seemingly incompatible emotions. Both deep gratitude for life and passionate grief, whether for another's or for one's own ending, are legitimate emotions held in tension.

Wrestling with this emotional tension brings me back again to Nelson's "body theology" and to an erotically informed ecology. What could be read as a contradiction in Nelson's latest book concerns me here. On the one hand, he is deeply convinced that "whenever we live as though death were the final word, we cultivate a life-style of death, indeed, a 'death-style.' ...We might then as well live for number one"; moreover, he believes that such a "death style is always deficient in compassion" and that it leads us to resent, even to punish, "everyone who reminds us too vividly that we too are mortal."[25] And yet, while he seems here to be denying that death is final for our embodied phenomenal selves, he also speaks in language consistent with that of both Ruether and Peters, albeit couched in more traditionally Christian terms, when he says, "The resurrection vision is not simply, or even primarily, a trust in an *individual's* survival after death. It is fundamentally a conviction of the profound unity and interconnectedness of all creation--in our birthings, in our illnesses, in our dyings, and in God's assurance that meaning will not be destroyed."[26]

Fortunately, we can discern some ways around this seeming contradiction: From an ecotheological perspective we can respond to Nelson that, yes, death *is* the final word for our individual, embodied, subjectively experiencing, phenomenal *selves*. At the same time, death is *not* the final word for our *lives* as "symbiotic unions of biology and culture" whose impact upon the relational web of Being continues affectively beyond our deaths. That we are not atomized and isolated individuals, but beings interwoven with/in/to Being provides an ethical mandate toward justice as right-relation, the same urging toward justice first experienced in erotic connectedness. As a result, even though death does have the final word for our phenomenal selves, we cannot live for number one in any reckless or irresponsible sense. Death's finality does not obviate human or environmental ethics.

"Living for number one" sounds a lot like "living as if there were no tomorrow," which is an expression we must turn on its head. For those of us living with HIV, or AIDS, or any other potentially life-threatening, chronic condition, we *must* live as if there were no tomorrow. We must *not* procrastinate, neglect, or deny. We must "seize the day" because we may not have tomorrow. This even strikes me as one of the more positive strands in New Testament eschatology: We are commanded to live in readiness for the *parousia*, for the very real possibility of our having no tomorrow. The significant qualifier here is that this is absolutely *not* an invitation to some otherworldly, ecologically disastrous eschaton; this is a demand to attend to *this* earth, *this* life, *these* relationships, because this is the only reality we can know. Carol Christ has elegantly insisted that "it is life that can end in death at any moment that we must love,"[27] and Nelson likewise concedes that "perhaps there is more capacity to be at home in this crazy, anxious, beautiful, violent, tender world precisely because we know that this [personal] life is fleeting [but] not final *in its meaning*,"[28] or, better said, its meaningful impact and influence on other life and other lives. We have to embrace both our gratitude and our grief.

As we open ourselves to life with gratitude and meet death with appropriate grief, knowing that life and death are really one, we can begin to take responsibility for our dying as well as for our living. Karl Peters encourages us to let go of our phenomenal selves, our subjective experiencing, at the point at which that letting go itself is required to enhance the quality of life, both for ourselves and for those others who most directly experience the impact of our living and dying. No heroic life-prolonging technology, please! For quality of *dying* and its impact on others, our unselfish letting go of our individual embodied lives and subjective experience can be a sacrificial, perhaps even sacramental, act on behalf of the quality of life for others. Then, like our births and our lives, death, too, becomes a "sacred event."[29] Indeed, we must find in our gratitude and wonder at this erotic and sensuous life the empowerment to trust *through* both our fear of the unknown and our grief at leaving embodied relationships and experiences, our grief that our subjective life must end, and thereby allow ourselves to be embraced anew by the divine oneness.

Nobody said it would be easy. But, a sweet bye-and-bye eschatology is not only escapism, but an escapism that impugns the earth and damages life with reckless, disvaluing disregard, and that, as a result, also threatens to deny the value of our personal lives as well. Rather than have the value of our lives so cancelled out, we can embrace our gratitude and our grief--our erotically embodied passions--and choose an absolutely trusting, eschatological leap of faith. It is a hard and painful choice, but it can also be a liberating and empowering one, freeing us from a fearful obsession with death to being more fully alive in the present. Says Ruether,[30]

> ...We can be confident that our creative work will be nourishing to the community of life, even as we relinquish our small self back into the great Self. Our final gesture, as we surrender ourself into the Matrix of life, then becomes a prayer [and an action] of ultimate trust.

The strength of our erotically empowered and embodied, loving relationships, our personal ecosystems if you will, can enable us into and through such a sacramental and sacred activity of passage.

3. Protest and Hope

When I first presented these ideas for an "ecology of dying" during a lecture at Union Theological Seminary in New York, my colleague Ron Long questioned the seemingly passive, even Pollyanish, acceptance of death and suffering he believed implicit in my remarks. His question reminded me that the question of theodicy--of human suffering and dying--has haunted my thinking for over two decades, from my undergraduate fascination with Alfred North Whitehead, to my more in-depth seminary studies of process theology, on into graduate school and several studies of the Holocaust. As a postdoctoral adult, suffering and dying, specifically from AIDS, have framed my work from the very beginning; my theological writing really began as a response to the first AIDS-death among my circle of friends.[31] Ron rightly perceived that, for the most part, I have resigned myself to a process theological perspective, believing the divine does all s/he can do in every instance, but acknowledging that that is often far from sufficient. Such a divine is not responsible for evil, or inbreaking chaos, but is too often impotent to save us from its consequences. In making a mental distinction, as a good process theologian should, between natural evil and human evil, I have been able to avoid blaming god/ess for the failed and perverted human responsibility of the Holocaust, racial lynchings, and anti-gay/lesbian violence. I have agreed with Dietrich Bonhoeffer that we must maturely assume responsibility for our actions, as if god/ess did not exist, conceding that the divine will not and cannot rescue us.[32] But, the loss of a compassionate *deus ex machina* in the face of a natural evil such as AIDS has left me grief-stricken. I feel as empty as I did the first Christmas after I learned there was no Santa Claus and before I could redirect those energies into being Santa Claus for my younger siblings. Though we may pick up the pieces and assume appropriate responsibility for being god/ess to one another and thereby for caring for one another during the AIDS pandemic, the absence of a rescuing divine remains a painfully felt reality.

Now, in my ecological work, death may make sense as part of the whole, but the question remains: "Why is there suffering at all?" It is very frightening to concede that there may be no answer. Ecologically speaking as a radical monotheist, I have come to see god/ess as the whole web of Being, as the cycles of life/death/rebirth, which clearly implicates the divine in both life and death--and we have to live in that paradox--but I also struggle with not making god/ess a culpable moral agent who either wills or allows our suffering. In wrestling with the dark side of the divine, and in turn with my own dark side, I have avoided assigning moral culpability to god/ess by always coming back to a process-informed, co-suffering, caring impotence. But that remains unsatisfying and Ron Long is correct in pointing out that I have not allowed myself to be angry about this state of theological and spiritual affairs. My southern Protestant upbringing taught me it wasn't *nice* to be angry. Indeed, in many southern families we are so busy being *nice*, we never get angry, and we never work through that anger to richer levels of intimacy in relation. Instead, anger turns inward to become resentment, or depression and low self-esteem, while our relationships are constituted by shallow pleasantries and distance rather than passionate confrontation and compassionate intimacy. And, of course, if one is not allowed to be angry at another person, one certainly is not allowed to be angry at the divine. That really wouldn't be *nice* and the angry person would probably go to hell!

Well, suffering *is* hell, a long and lingering AIDS-death is hell, grieving homophobic oppression and anti-gay/lesbian violence year after year is hell, losing dozens and dozens of our friends to AIDS is hell. And we should be mad as hell. I should be. Ron Long reminded me again that, particularly in the Jewish side of my mixed bag of faith development, our tradition says it's o.k. to get mad at the divine. I have learned to trust the intimate relationship with my spouse to the extent that I can be angry with him or he can be angry with me, yet we know we still love each other. I must learn to have no less faith in my relationship to the divine; but that is a very scary act of faith, one neither passive nor Pollyanish, and one which requires some special resources.

Elie Wiesel has articulated my dilemma well in his marvelous play, *The Trial of God*, wherein the evil of pogroms and the righteousness of protest are played out.[33] Wiesel reminds us that to deny the existence of the divine because of suffering and death implies a kind of answer to theodicy, when in fact no answer may exist and "everything remains hidden."[34] Likewise, there are times when trying to separate human evil and natural evil, to focus on human responsibility and to soften our anger at the divine just doesn't work. Wiesel reminds us that *both* kinds of evil implicate god/ess, when Berish, his protesting innkeeper declares, "Every man [*sic.*] who suffers or causes suffering, every woman who is raped, every child who is tormented implicates" the divine.[35] Both the fag-basher and AIDS implicate god/ess.

Through the character of Berish, Wiesel wisely articulates both our questions and our frustrations: We desperately want an answer to theodicy which we can understand, a conception of divine justice which makes sense of our everyday understandings of what justice means; but, no such answer comes.[36] God/ess conceptualized as a neutral bystander to suffering isn't enough, nor is an impotent, limited, process deity.[37] Can we then find any satisfaction in seeing the divine as less present in the causes of suffering and more present as advocate of the victims of suffering?[38] Will an empathetic and co-suffering, but basically powerless, divine work to skirt theodicy? Is the impotence of process still a kind of divine complicity in evil? But, do we, Job-like, have any better reality from which to choose?

The god of the whirlwind did not *really* answer Job, but both the Job-writer and Wiesel insist that protest against the no-answer is the only response which allows us both our dignity and our human(e)ity. As Berish puts it, "I have not opted for God. I'm against his [*sic.*] enemies, that's all."[39] In fact, to defend our traditional concepts of an all-powerful, all-loving, all-knowing divine, a divine whose justice is not ours to understand, may well be to play into the hands of evil itself. In the play's surprising final action, Wiesel reminds us that God and Satan are in cohoots, tormenting Job. The defender of God is (un)masked as the Devil himself, reiterating the innkeeper's truth that protest is the *real* act of faith.[40]

Not unlike Wiesel, biblical theologian Tom Milazzo asks, "Can we love a God that is silent in the presence of our death? ...That does nothing to prevent our suffering?"[41]

He argues that suffering reveals not the vivid clarity of the divine, but divine ambiguity, the both/and of presence/absence and certainly the absence of rescue.[42] Moreover, any satisfactory answer to the theodicy question also "remains inaccessible"; there is no resolution to theodicy.[43] And, again as for Wiesel, this unsatisfactory reality becomes the foundation for Milazzo's action of faith and protest, grounded in the Wisdom tradition of scripture:[44]

> We are to live, as brief as that life may be. ...This is all we can do. [For Qoheleth] this confidence is an act of faith and trust in God.
>
> ...Only because there is love and faith can there be a protest against a fate that, however human, is most inhumane. ...[The] protest against death ... stands as a mark of all that is human.

Reviewing my own theological development in light of Long's pointed questions, Milazzo's biblical theology, and Wiesel's dramatic presentation, helps me to re-articulate my own faith-response to theodicy. They help me to know which questions to ask and to realize there are far more questions than answers; they also help me to know how to be angry, how to protest, and thereby how to act in faith.

To lament the absence of god/ess as rescuer from suffering and tragedy also entails protesting that abandonment. Grief entails anger and protest toward the reality that this is just the way it is--period. Anger and grief go hand in hand, as they do for the child who has temporarily lost its parents (experienced as being abandoned by them) in a large store. Our unanswered lament (our plea and our protest) in the face of that abandonment and in the face of the negatives of life (suffering) both heightens the preciousness of life's goods and undermines our experience of thanksgiving for those goods. How can we be grateful to one who abandons us? Is the divine only a fair-weather friend? Or, not really there at all? How do we direct our prayers, whether of gratitude or anger, to an amorphous, ecologically whole web of Being? We are left again with the paradoxical mixture of both gratitude (as joy and thanksgiving) and grief (as mourning and angry protest) before a reality we cannot change and without any answerable, theistic being.

Although suffering (the dying process) remains my primary concern (and, ecologically speaking, for all life), the idea that death is not-being also troubles me. I, too, resist mortality. But, why do we crave eternal life, life in relation, in relation to this ambiguous divine? Why do we need eternity to justify our present? Why can't we simply relate to the divine within our temporal, ecological limitations, within our mortality? The eschatological leap of faith is no easier than the faith required for protest. I don't want to be separated from life and relationships and nature and god/ess. But if the cycles of life/death, interwoven with/in/to the whole web of Being (an ecological divine oneness), are all there is and if in death there is no subjective experience of these separations, what does my resisting mortality mean, except, tautologically, that I don't want these experiences to end? My passing into nonbeing does not invalidate or cancel my having been. Mortality does not erase the reality and value of the humanity we are, albeit for a finite time. That finitude notwithstanding, our lives affect the ongoingness of life and, for that reason, my bottom line value remains that of enhancing the quality of life for all life, whether or not an answerable, humanly satisfactory divine even exists. That value is my assumption of responsibility, my *tikkun olam*, my faith.

Celebrating life and pursuing quality of life do not, of course, preclude mortality. Perhaps, regardless of how unfair it seems, mortality really isn't unfair. Death isn't a blame issue; it's merely a value-neutral given. To be human is to be mortal. Faith depends upon our humanity, our response-ability, which necessarily entails our finitude. Perhaps, suffering, like death, is merely a given, something value-neutral which we nonetheless experience as unfair, unjust, and evil. I know my mortality is real, I know my suffering from anti-gay/lesbian exclusion is real, I know the suffering of AIDS-death is real. And I don't like this reality! These things will not be "eclipsed" or justified by eternity.[45] I may not like the failure of the divine to prevent or to rescue from suffering, but even in my anger and protest, I recognize that such "divine impotence" or *absence* need not preclude divine cosmic caring or *presence* as well--a frustrating both/and. My awareness of something in the mystery and ambiguity (in the darkness, the absence, the impotence) and a belief that this something cares both enables and sustains my life. Like the ambiguous divine, then, my faith is both affirming this reality of caring and angrily protesting this reality of suffering. Indeed, refusing to be defeated by suffering and death (not giving up or giving in) is my assertion of human dignity, my action or embodiment of faith. We have to live in paradox, with ambiguity, because liberation theology also teaches us that, by our (inter)actions of justice as right-relation to both humans and nonhumans, we bring god/ess into being, which in turn empowers us, while our failures to so act diminish the divine in our midst. The ebb and flow of presence and absence, of joy and suffering, of responsibility and irresponsibility, of gratitude, and anger and grief, these things cannot be separated!

What I want, then, is to make sure that I have affected other life (both human and nonhuman) in such a way as to enhance the quality of other life and then to have some way to make the transition from individual being (from my subjective experience) into collective nonbeing (death) with integrity and dignity, and with the love of god/ess, trustworthy in anger and in gratitude, embodied in my spouse and in my friends, all of whom will be there for me, both through any suffering I must undergo and at the point of my departure. That is my faith, my style of resisting, and my hope.[46]

4. A Metaphor of Wholeness

As I have wrestled with these concerns, I have become more and more willing to argue that our best understanding of the divine is one which insists that god/ess is interwoven into and through all that is; all the individual expressions of life together constitute the divine. Just as we experience a relationship over time as something over and above the two individuals in that relationship, god/ess is something that includes all that is but which, as the whole-cloth of all that is, cannot be simplistically reduced to the parts. The metaphor which has consistently come to mind is that of a quilt. A quilt is made up of various pieces of fabric, different designs, different textures, which must be sewn together into a whole-cloth for the quilt to exist. A simple pile of swatches of cloth (a simple total of the parts) does not make a quilt, but their *interrelatedness* into a whole does. Each piece of the quilt is a part of the whole-cloth, just as each living thing is a part of the divine. Just as "quiltness" is a part of each piece of a quilt once it is sewn into the whole, so the divine is interwoven into and through each individual life which participates in the whole of life, of Being itself. Every individual life, both human and nonhuman, geospheric and biospheric, embodies or incarnates the divine.

This also means there is no first cause, no divine quilt maker. The cosmic quilt did not originate outside itself. There is no creator God in this traditional sense. Unlike humanly crafted quilts, the cosmic quilt just is. And, as a result, good and evil are not warring opposites in the fabric of life. Good and evil constitute a unity, not a dualism. Reality simply is. Sometimes the fabric in a particular swatch of cloth is weaker than that in other swatches; sometimes the threads which bind piece to piece are not as sturdy. As the life of the quilt progresses, those weaker pieces tear; they undergo suffering. And, surrounding swatches are diminished by the loss of their weakened and "suffering" neighbors; humanly speaking, they undergo grief. But the suffering and the grieving which the pieces of the quilt experience are not imposed from outside; they are not caused by some moral agent, some supreme quilter who purposefully chose weak fabric or sloppy stitching. Although I may *protest* against this reality, I cannot *blame* the fabric of life for the fact that I will not last forever, but I can rejoice that, because the quilt of life is *organic*, as I pass out of existence, other pieces of life-fabric will be born and will grow into their rightful, although equally transient, places within the quilt. Importantly, as well, the whole-cloth does not punish some swatches or patterns for differing from other swatches or patterns. Diversity is the very richness of the quilt.

And so, I find myself trying to affirm that both good and evil, life and death, even death from HIV progression and AIDS, are simply part and parcel of the whole. I may not like that reality, but I cannot escape it. We have erred whenever we have conceptualized the divine as a moral agent who was anthropomorphically assigned all power, all knowledge, and all goodness. We have erred whenever we expected the divine to act, morally good, as a rescuer. We have erred whenever we blamed the divine for acting, morally bad, as the cause of so called natural evil. And, we have also erred whenever we accused the divine of weakness, moral or otherwise, for failing to rescue us from reality, however difficult to bear it may be. While human evil (injustice) rightly demands human correctives, natural evil and suffering are our experiences of natural processes which are really, in and of themselves, morally neutral components of a morally neutral and given whole-cloth, however grievous those processes and experiences may be to us. This is not to deny the reality and the pathos of our experience. Our pain, our grief, our suffering, and our deaths are certainly real. Indeed, even though natural evils do not have any ultimate Final Cause, these occasions demand appropriate human response, which is to say: compassion. In and of itself, HIV is also morally neutral. Our experience of its activity in our bodies and our experience of the ways in which it brings many of us to premature ends are together something which we certainly experience as evil, and we rightly protest its reality and struggle to find ways to overcome its power. But we cannot blame the divine for its existence; rather, we must turn our ethical considerations toward those humans who use this occurrence of experienced natural evil as occasions for enacting human evil, human hatred, and human injustice.

Carol Christ has said that she believes that "all that is cares."[47] Ron Long has argued that the divine is not a creator, or even a personal being, but is best understood as resistance (to human injustice and to occurrences of natural evil) and as hope (in the fulfilling of human justice and in the overcoming of human suffering).[48] I have tried to synthesize these ideas.[49] I know that god/ess is not a being as such, not a creator, not a first mover, or a divine quiltmaker. Rather, the divine is interwoven with/in/to the very fabric of life; s/he is the whole-cloth of Being itself, the organic quilting of all that is. And yet, I believe that we often *experience* this as personal, as if god/ess in godself was still someone with whom we could relate, with whom we could enter into dialogue in prayer or worship. I have wanted to exculpate this anthropomorphic image of the divine from responsibility for evil, as if the divine and evil were separable, but my own radical monotheism will not allow such dualism. Nevertheless, I still "experience" the divine as companion, friend, co-creator and co-sufferer, as comfort in suffering and empowerment in the pursuit of justice.[50]

Perhaps the quilt image will help again. As one swatch within the fabric of life, I can speak of the whole, not as something objectified outside myself (as an I-It relation), but as the whole of which I am intimately a part (as an I-Thou relation). To speak of and even to the whole, metaphorically as if it were not-me, does not mean that I do not recognize that I am a part of that whole-cloth with whom I commune in meditation or prayer, or about whom I speak theologically. The divine is as intimately interwoven with/in/to my being as I am with/in/to godself. The web of Being changes and we undergo suffering and even death, but the cosmic whole-cloth is organic and lives on. New lives come into being. Our lives and our deaths are a part of that whole. We bear responsibilities to be the best we can be within that whole, to contribute well to the quality of the relationships, the ties that bind us, within that whole. That responsibility, that demand for justice as right-relation, is not limited merely to our sexual partners or to other humans; it is an ecological demand: The very givenness of the quilt of life, the sacred fabric of Being, demands our just caring, cooperation, and responsibility for all the rest of the fabric, whether human or nonhuman, biospheric or geospheric, for each individual piece that, like ourselves, contributes to the rich diversity of the whole. Surely, in enacting and embodying right-relation within the whole, we strengthen the whole, we add to its diversity, we give it life. We are with-god/ess even as we experience god/ess-with-us through all the cycles of life and death. Evolving together. One.

---

[1] The major contributors to this synthesis are: Carter Heyward, *Our Passion for Justice: Images of Power, Sexuality, and Liberation* (New York: Pilgrim Press, 1984), and, *Touching our Strength: The Erotic as Power and the Love of God* (San Francisco: Harper, 1989); James B. Nelson, *Between Two Gardens: Reflections on Sexuality and Religious Experience* (New York: Pilgrim Press, 1983), *The Intimate Connection: Male Sexuality, Masculine Spirituality* (Philadelphia: Westminster Press, 1988), and, *Body Theology* (Louisville: Westminster/John Knox Press, 1992).

[2] Nelson, *Body Theology*, p. 186.

[3] Nelson, *Between Two Gardens*, p. 13; *Body Theology*, pp. 45, 116-117.

[4] Nelson, *Body Theology*, p. 43.

[5] Anne Primavesi, *From Apocalypse to Genesis: Ecology, Feminism and Christianity* (Minneapolis: Augsburg Fortress Press, 1991), p. 54.

[6] J. Michael Clark, *Beyond our Ghettos: Gay Theology in Ecological Perspective* (Cleveland: Pilgrim Press, 1993), pp. 12-20, 88-90; and, J. Michael Clark, "From Gay Men's Lives: Toward a More Inclusive, Ecological Vision," *Journal of Men's Studies* 1.4 (May 1993), pp. 347-358; the ensuing discussion represents excerpts and

summaries of the analytical paradigm originally put forth in these previously published resources.

[7] Primavesi, *From Apocalypse to Genesis*, p. 156.

[8] Marti Kheel, "Ecofeminism and Deep Ecology: Reflections on Identity and Difference," *Reweaving the World: The Emergence of Ecofeminism* (I. Diamond and G.F. Orenstein, eds.; San Francisco: Sierra Club Books, 1990), pp. 128-137.

[9] J. Michael Clark, *A Place to Start: Toward an Unapologetic Gay Liberation Theology* (Dallas: Monument Press, 1989), pp. 45-52, 65-78, 164-175; Ronald E. Long and J. Michael Clark, *AIDS, God, and Faith: Continuing the Dialogue on Constructing Gay Theology* (Dallas: Monument Press, 1992).

[10] Primavesi, *From Apocalypse to Genesis*, p. 43.

[11] *Ibid.*, p. 22.

[12] Roger S. Gottlieb, "Weapons of the Spirit: Jewish Resources in the Struggle against the Environmental Crisis," unpublished paper, roundtable presentation, American Academy of Religion, Kansas City, 25 November 1991.

[13] Catherine Keller, "Women Against Wasting the World: Notes on Eschatology and Ecology," *Reweaving the World*, p. 257.

[14] Karl E. Peters, "Ethics of Dying in Light of a Social Ecological Understanding of Human Nature," unpublished paper, roundtable presentation, American Academy of Religion, San Francisco, 23 November 1992, p. 8.

[15] *Ibid.*, p. 7.

[16] *Ibid.*, p. 5.

[17] Rosemary Radford Ruether, *Gaia and God: An Ecofeminist Theology of Earth Healing* (San Francisco: Harper, 1992), p. 251.

[18] *Ibid.*, p. 53.

[19] Peters, "Ethics of Dying," p. 4.

[20] *Ibid.*, p. 2.

[21] Ruether, *Gaia and God*, p. 71, cf., pp. 208-220.

[22] *Ibid.*, p. 139.

[23] Peters, "Ethics of Dying," p. 7.

[24] *Ibid.*, pp. 12, 16, emphasis added.

[25] Nelson, *Body Theology*, p. 176.

[26] *Ibid.*, p. 134, emphasis added.

[27] Carol P. Christ, "Rethinking Theology and Nature," *Reweaving the World*, p. 67.

[28] Nelson, *Body Theology*, p. 90, emphasis added.

[29] Peters, "Ethics of Dying," p. 19, cf., p. 18f.

[30] Ruether, *Gaia and God*, p. 253.

[31] J. Michael Clark, "AIDS, Death, and God: Gay Liberational Theology and the Problem of Suffering," *Journal of Pastoral Counseling* 21.1 (1986): 40-54, and, "Special Considerations in Pastoral Care of Gay Persons with AIDS, *Journal of Pastoral Counseling* 22.1 (1987): 32-45.

[32] Dietrich Bonhoeffer, *Letters and Papers from Prison*, ed. Eberhard Bethge (New York: Macmillan Co, 1953), p. 196.

[33] Elie Wiesel, *The Trial of God*, trans. M. Wiesel (1979. New York: Schocken Books, 1986).

[34] *Ibid*., p. 89, cf., pp. 26, 85.

[35] *Ibid*., p. 54.

[36] *Ibid*., p. 123.

[37] *Ibid*., p. 128.

[38] *Ibid*., p. 129.

[39] *Ibid*., p. 156, cf., 132, 133.

[40] *Ibid*., pp. 160-161.

[41] G. Tom Milazzo, *The Protest and the Silence: Suffering, Death, and Biblical Theology* (Minneapolis: Fortress Press, 1992), p. x.

[42] *Ibid*., p. 33, cf., p. 46.

[43] *Ibid*., p. 86.

[44] *Ibid*., pp. 134, 167.

[45] Cf., *ibid*., p. 136.

[46] Cf., Ronald E. Long, "God through Gay Men's Eyes: Gay Theology in the Age of AIDS," *AIDS, God, and Faith*, pp. 15-18.

[47] Carol P. Christ, "Rethinking Theology and Nature," *Reweaving the World*, p. 69.

[48] Ronald E. Long, "God through Gay Men's Eyes: Gay Theology in the Age of AIDS," *AIDS, God, and Faith*, pp. 15-18.

[49] J. Michael Clark, "Toward a Lavender Credo: From Theology to Belief," *AIDS, God, and Faith*, pp. 51-55.

[50] *Ibid*., pp. 54-55, cf., 77-80.

Ronald E. Long

Toward a Phenomenology of Gay Sex:
Groundwork for a Contemporary Sexual Ethic

---

1. Introduction

It is only recently that observers of the gay community were claiming that, under the threat of AIDS, gay men were abandoning their "promiscuous" ways in favor of sex within relational intimacy, and that the hedonistic ethic of the 70's was being replaced by an ethic of "constraint and commitment."[1] What such commentators on the gay scene had not counted on was the fact that gay desire for "promiscuous" sex was not to disappear. If relational, monogamous sex had become the only sex that was at all safe, then gays were willing to bite the bullet and, as a way to energize the renunciation of their earlier ways, confess how "sinful" they had been. But, when more became known about the actual processes of HIV infection, and it became clear that there could be such a thing as relatively safe casual sex, J/O clubs and sex parties appeared to replace the baths that had been closed. And the hunt for tricks in the bars returned with renewed energy. It is as if the urge to "fuck around" had only been lying in wait, ready to express itself as soon as it became a prudent possibility. What is the significance of sex, and in particular of sex outside of intimate relations,[2] for gay men?

Reflecting on the "remarkable qualities of communication with men whose names he never knew, men with whom he may not even have had sex, men whom he embraced and then moved on" in that temple of trick sex--the baths--Armistead Maupin confided in an interview with Frank Browning that it was then that he felt "'very close to God.'"[3] Another gay man, Bruce Boone, told him that "the first time you suck dick, it really is like Holy Communion."[4] Browning says that he eventually came to discover that the association between sex and God is "extraordinarily common" among gay men. What is extraordinarily common among gay men, however, is not finally explicable through the resources of our tradition. Barring the not very helpful approach of Plato (and perhaps Solovyov), and whatever might be gleaned from the use of religious imagery in the tradition of romance,[5] the resources of the Western tradition proffer precious little for those who would understand the spiritual dimensions of sex, for sustained phenomenological attention to sex remains one of the glaring lacunae in our inherited analyses.

The theological tradition in particular, it seems to me, has proven itself to be more interested in legislation and control than in understanding. With regard to sexual ethics, we can profitably distinguish between two basic approaches. One approach would first decide what sex is for, and then use the discerned "point" of sex as the principle for ethical discrimination. In the other approach (tracing its lineage back to the Aristotle of *The Nichomachean Ethics*), one looks at what people actually do, trying to discern the point of their *praxis* so as to help them more directly "hit their mark." It is the former approach that has characterized Christian sexual ethics even until the present. Early Christianity, especially in its Augustinian form, saw in sex a threat to rational self-control--the essence of saintliness--and could only authorize such dangerous self-indulgence within the bonds of matrimony *and* for the sake of procreation. Sex was at best a necessary evil in fulfilling the divine ordinance to "fill the earth." The Reformers, of course, toyed with the idea that marriage might be for the purposes of companionship as well as for procreation. Following their lead, contemporary religious thinking has come so to link sex with companionate intimacy that sex in any other context, except as accommodation to dire necessity, is viewed as ethically problematic.

Such a conjunction of sexual with relational intimacy characterizes recent developments in gay-sympathetic Christian sexual ethics and extends even into the growing iteration of lesbian and gay theology. The late Andre Guindon, for example, in his efforts to clear the ground for the acceptance of gay sex on par with heterosexual sex within the parameters of Catholic tradition, argued that sex is the "language" of intimacy, and that its use to say anything else is to misspeak.[6] Lesbian feminist Carter Heyward insists that committed friendship is the appropriate context of sex,[7] while her colleague Mary Hunt sees friendship as the relation that invites and authorizes sex.[8] Gay theologian J. Michael Clark--while allowing that gays might legitimately indulge in promiscuous sex, a kind of "making up for lost time," when they come out--holds that there comes a time when gays ought to get serious and restrict themselves to the real business of sex--and that is as an affair for intimates.[9] Since right relation (for Heyward and Clark) and friendship (for Hunt) are actualizations of the divine, they are able to see intimate sex as "of God." It is surprising to me that the lesbian theologians Heyward and Hunt prove the more revolutionary here, in that they envision the possibility of sexual friends in the plural, whereas Guindon and Clark tend to see intimacy as an affair of couples. Most gay men that I know, on the other hand, can divide their social partners into lovers, friends, and "tricks"--these last being those whom we team up with only for sex, usually in one night stands. Although some gays may have "fuck buddies," people they would get together with regularly for sex, fuck buddies are still not sexual friends in the full sense that Heyward uses the term. In the 70's, it was almost axiomatic that one did not have sex with friends. The late Michael Callen has recently argued that sex is now seen as possible between friends.[10] However, tricking continues to occupy a privileged position in the sex life of the gay community. Our regnant ethical discourse would render such sex ethically questionable, and devoid of spiritual maturity. Yet it is precisely such sex that is included, if not singled out, when gay men say that sex constitutes for them a religious experience.

In what follows, I propose to initiate an "Aristotelian" study of gay tricking, seeking to understand the meaning it has for gay men as evidenced in their praxis.[11] I do not presume to know what kind of sex all gay men have; and my study is restricted to gay tricking, an institution characteristic of gay life in the urban ghettos. It is hoped that phenomenological attention to gay tricking will suggest the contours of an appropriate and contemporary viable gay sexual ethic, as well as contribute to an appreciation of the spiritual dimension of sex[12] in general. Specifically, I will be concerned with two issues--one negative, one positive. First of all, the account will provide grounds for setting aside the popular assumption that having sex with someone with whom one is not antecedently on intimate terms is a matter of ethical abuse, in common parlance, a matter of "using" another as a "sex object."[13] The phrasing that would make non-intimate sex a matter of "using another as a (sex) object" calls to mind the Kantian injunction that it is inappropriate to "use" another person as anything other than as an end in him/herself, namely as a "object" or means to one's own gratification. If one were to insist that non-intimate sex is appropriately characterized as "using another as a sex object," I would argue that the interpretation of such "use" of another as a matter of abuse proceeds by way of an equivocal use of the word "object." But I really want to challenge the characterization of non-intimate sex as matter of "using" of another as an "object." Such phrasing implies that tricking is necessarily an act of de-personalization and de-humanization of another, whereas I will attempt to show that tricking is a matter of interpersonal treasuring and veneration. Tricking may become ethically abusive, but only if other factors intrude; it is not abusive in and of itself.

On a positive note, if we can distance ourselves from the notion that sex with someone outside of a committed--or even an emerging committed--relation is ethically problematic, then we can likewise move on to reconfigure the way we think about sex and intimacy. If sex is only legitimate as the symbol and vehicle of relational intimacy, then sex outside of a committed relation is somehow distorted. But if we can begin to see that intimacy is but one mode of relation which sex may betoken, then we are freed to perceive meaning(s) that sex can carry independent of its subservience to relational intimacy. Indeed, I will be making a case for thinking of sex between committed intimates as a cultivated form of the interrelating that is true of sex in general, whether within a committed relation or no.

In formulating the project in this way, I am of course assuming there is a meaning, an intentional structure, which can be discerned in sex. I am fully aware of the multiplicity of meanings which sex can have for different people and for the same people at different moments in their life. The sex that I have after I get a job is a different kind of sex than the kind I have after I have been fired; the sex I have with my "first love" may be different than the sex I have with a lover of ten years. Yet all these meanings may concur with and be built upon a common basal meaning. But how do we get at such a meaning, particularly since sex is proverbially one part biology and nine parts imagination? I do not propose to make this a narrowly psychological study, nor will I be relying on what people say sex means or has meant to them in confession or poetic evocation. Rather I will be looking at what people do, what they say, the demeanor of their bodies, and how they go about this business of sex. I will try to be attentive to the conventions of tricking as a clue to what kind of experience such conventions both facilitate and foster. The question will be, what must be going on here if this is the way people are interacting?

2. Tricking: Phenomenological Account of a Night Out

a. Preliminaries

I propose, then, we begin by following a young man as he goes out one Friday night. Our young man lives in one of the urban gay ghettos in one of America's gay "meccas"--New York, let us say. He is probably white and middle class. Although he might spend a lot of summer weekends and/or vacation time in one of the gay resorts like Cherry Grove or The Pines on Fire Island, he is probably not so affluent that he has not had to save his pennies to do so. His work may or may not be in one of the stereotypical gay careers, such as work in the arts or in the design industry, or in a hair salon--but his social life will be centered in the gay community and the gay ghetto. Now, it's Friday night, and the work week is over. Although he is tempted to stay home and watch TV, he decides that he wants to be around people who are not his work mates--and besides, he might get laid! A gay bar offers just the thing, a place where he might see some friends and where other guys who hope they might get laid are gathering. As he enters the bar, the knowledge that sex is in the air--that is, that here might be a prospective mate for the night--is enough to work a bodily effect. The prospect of sex brings with it heightened awareness of the sensitivity of the skin and a certain tightness to the muscles, reminiscent of the fitness or readiness of an athlete before a game. Our young man is scarcely aware of it except as a kind of nervous energy.

At the bar, he sees some friends of his, greets them with a kiss and a hug, and is brought into the conversation. Such conversation may even be characterized by a high degree of camp. The guys may well refer to each other or to others with the feminine pronouns "she" and "her." So, too, the conversants may gesture "effeminately." (Actors are good guides here to gestures, movements, and stances that are "read" as stereotypically feminine or masculine.) The conversation will not generally be so engrossing that each of the conversants may not be also glancing around the room to see who is there. And they will be quite free, having noticed a particularly attractive man, to turn to one another and say, "Wow! Did you see that one?"--or words to that effect. However, no matter how much he has been camping around, when our young man turns his attention to seeking out a sex partner--as distinct from merely noticing others--

he will "butch up his act." He may choose to "go for a walk," cruising the bar. Or he may position himself apart from his friends in a characteristic cruising pose. (In a typical cruising pose, the weight is unevenly distributed between the feet; the body is slightly contraposto, since the man will be leaning against a wall or a bar; the arms might be crossed--or the thumb of one hand might be hooked around a belt loop or in a pocket so that the other fingers seem to point to the crotch.) To be sure, the walk and/or the posing signal to the environing others that our young man is interested in and might be receptive to sexual advances. But he is not merely signaling a general sexual receptivity, but is also presenting himself, displaying himself, in stereotypically masculine posture, gesture, and demeanor. Our young man is not merely signaling interest in sex, but is seeking to make himself sexually attractive by "advertising" his masculinity. The conventions of cruising testify that, within the world of the bars at least, sexual attractiveness inheres in masculine styling, presentation, and display.

In our culture, imbued with its traditions of discriminating appearance and reality, we are all to apt to dismiss such self-presentation as "mere" posturing, as nothing but costume and/or disguise. However, if gender lay in the "styling" of a sexed body, then "posing" masculinely can be revelatory, authentic self-display. It is commonplace to distinguish between "sex" and "gender": our "sex" commonly refers to the biological condition of being male or female, while our "gender" is usually understood to be our (actual or expected) way of living as male or female in the world. If we can refrain from following Judith Butler's (post-modernist?) dismissal of gender ideals as pure artifice, as but "camp," her suggestion that gender be understood as the "effect" of an habitual and habituated performance is fruitful here.[14] To speak of gender as "performance" is to invoke a theatrical metaphor. When thinking of an actor's performance, we can focus on his "role," the things he is scripted to do or say, or we may think of his performance style, the way in which the role is enacted. And performance style in turn can refer either to the actor's personal relation to his role (*i.e.*, whether he plays his part hesitantly, whole-heartedly, haltingly) or the styling of the role itself (*i.e.*, whether the part is played broadly, comically, melodramatically). It is unclear to me whether sexual attractiveness ("sexiness") is attributed *despite* gender role expectation (as in the case of the woman who laments how unfortunate it is that the hunk near the punch bowl is gay)--or *independently* of gender role ("See that hunk over there--I wonder if he's gay or straight"). But I do want to argue that sexual attractiveness is more a matter of style than of role. Indeed, it seems to me that male sexual attractiveness lies, principally, in the presentational intensity of a masculinely cultivated body, where "masculine" cultivation or styling refers to ways of accentuating or complementing the maleness of the male. Richard Mohr has written:[15]

> Since biological sex pervades the whole appearance of a male, the male body, sexed all over as a subject, provides a highly determinate natural substrate with specific capacities for development of the male into a nonarbitrary masculine. When masculine presentations build on or actualize natural male capacities, the scents and forms of man, rather than being merely an array of arbitrary conventions and signs, they issue in the hypermasculine--a threshold-crossing intensification of the masculine. This natural but developed masculine body provides, in turn, a natural object for possible ... male homoeroticism.

Where Mohr speaks of the "hypermasculine," I would prefer speaking of the "masculinely styled male," or even the "impressively male." It seems to me that it is not masculinity as such that is attractive, but rather an individual male masculinely cultivated and displayed.[16] My point is an Aristotelian one, that masculinity does not exist ontologically apart from its embodiment in the body of a person; and I would emphasize further the importance of the male body, masculinely cultivated, as the focus of erotic interest. Masculine cultivation augments and thus intensifies the maleness of the male body.

Gay men who flock to the gyms to "get in shape" know this intuitively. They seek less to get "fit" than to get shapely. And they know that it is gym-training, not tennis, that effects the muscular development of which males are uniquely capable. It is not that tennis is unmanly--the role does not make or unmake the man--but tennis is not a mode of "masculine" physical culture in the sense of the present discussion. And as our young man at the bar evidences, men on the make also know that masculine display enhances sexual attractiveness. No matter how much camping around a man may do with friends in a gay bar, when he seeks to attract a sexual partner, he will "butch up his act"--that is, he will assume a masculine style of stance, carriage, and behavior. That is to say, masculine styling is a mode of displaying the self in and through the way one has cultivated the body and the way in which one stands, moves, and acts.

Such masculine styling becomes authentic display, rather than mere posing and posturing, to the extent it prove consistently thorough-going, habitual, and unforced. In gay argot one of the standing laments is "I thought he was so hot--but he proved such a lady!"[17] What is expected--what constitutes being sexually "hot"--is a seemingly thoroughgoing and consistent masculinity. One's looks cannot be masculine and one's voice feminine. At the same time, one's masculine styling must be so habitual that, however one might deviate for a moment, one's masculinity is what impresses itself on the other. Lastly, one's masculine styling must be "natural" in the sense of being unforced. The choice to discuss sports in a gay bar, for example, may very well compromise one's attractiveness. It is not that discussing sports is unmasculine, for indeed sports is the *lingua franca* of males in modern American culture. But choosing to discuss sports in the context of a gay bar may indicate to the environing others that, just like the actor who performs his role uncomfortably, one is trying too hard to be butch. Macho swaggering is not attractive--security in the masculine role is. In short, masculinity is the perceived effect of a consistent, seamless, unforced styling. When "masculinity" --even though styled--appears natural and native to the individual, the individual is seen as a "hunk."[18]

b. Foreplay

To use the vernacular, "it takes two to tango"--a sexual encounter is more than a matter of being attractive or of finding another attractive. A sexual affair is interactive. Whether our young man catches another's eye after having self-consciously positioned himself in a "come on" pose which signals his receptivity to sexual overtures, or whether he catches another's glance by accident, as it were, it is the "cruise" that changes a situation from one of general sociality to a definitely sexual one. While our young man is still primarily engaged in conversation with his friends, he will be free to say to his friends--as we have stated before--

"Wow! Did you see that one over there?" if he has chanced to spy a particularly good-looking man. A cruise, however, changes the social dynamics. Our subject will no longer feel free to turn to his friends and say "Wow! Look who's looking at me!"--unless, of course, he is sure that he is not interested in the guy cruising him. To do so breaks the spell of "privatization" which the cruise casts.[19] Indeed, a sexual scenario involves a bracketing of the everyday and everyday sociality, a focusing of attentiveness in which ordinary sociality is felt as an interruption or intrusion.

A "cruise" is a particular kind of look. Someone merely looking at me is not cruising me. The cruise is a look that announces desire and invites a similar response. Ordinarily, if I happen to catch someone looking at me, I will probably glance away almost immediately. On the other hand, there is a compulsion in the cruise that holds my gaze for a fraction of a second longer than is socially acceptable in almost any other context. Looking each other in the eye is usually either an act of aggression--pugilists will try to stare each other down prior to an event--or an effort to engage the other. It is socially exceptional. And even now, one or the other of the cruising parties will avert his eyes. Whatever elements of habit and shame may be involved here, gazing too long would also have the effect of contracting with the other prematurely. Averting the gaze after a moment sets into motion a rhythmic dance of intimacy.

In the view being presented here, a sexual encounter is an interaction that passes through three overlapping phases, each characterized by a different rhythmic interplay. The first phase constitutes a mutual introduction during which the partners draw together and pull apart as a way of testing each other's interest in the other--both assuring themselves of their own interest in the other and in the other's interest in them. The second phase is constituted by a rhythm of touch in which each is persuaded by the other to abandon "everyday consciousness" for what I will call "body consciousness." The third phase is taken up by the rhythm of thrusting and withdrawal that is intercourse, a process which centers the self in and on the genitalia. This phase is succeeded (or shall we say, climaxed) by the autonomous rhythmic spasms of ejaculation.

Averting the gaze, as I have suggested, sets into motion the rhythmics of introduction. The withdrawal of gaze gives the parties time to assure themselves that the other is truly attractive to them, in which case they will find their eyes being drawn back to the person again and again. To find the other's eyes being drawn back to me, on the other hand, assures me of the depth of his attraction to me. Good sex requires a reciprocity of interest. At the same time, if the one who holds my gaze looks too long and/or too hard, his desire will seem not so much desire as desperate neediness. His attractiveness will be compromised, and I will experience his desire as threatening assault. If I am not finally attracted, any further glancing in his direction will be a way of checking whether the "threat" is still there.

After a while, a threshold will be crossed in which each will recognize that an approach to each other will be mutually welcomed. Since the other is after all a stranger, it is the game of cruising that assures me of the safety which the depth of his desire guarantees. If our bar setting does not have a back room where things might proceed to the physical without intervening discussion, verbal intercourse will precede the physical. The game of mutual staring will be ended with a smile and a nod, and our couple will approach one another and begin to speak. But the game--the simultaneous testing of one another's attraction and attractiveness--continues, and is perhaps the real point of whatever is said.

This is not to say that the content of conversation is irrelevant. There are conventions at work here. "One such convention," observes Richard Mohr, "is that, in the conversations one conducts while picking one up in a gay bar, one is expected to present oneself at the lowest common intellectual denominator and not to press to discover the other person's occupation."[20] Indeed, in the context of picking someone up, the response to the question "What do you do?" may very well be confusion, since it will not be clear whether the question involves how one makes his living or what one likes to do in bed. The convention is instructive, since it testifies that, in picking someone up, one is not really interested in the other in the historical density of the other as full individual. Some observers would take this mutually honored reserve of aspects of the self as evidence of "de-personalization." We must tread carefully here lest we label as "de-personalizing" the way people in fact become personally present and involved in social settings. The "frame analysis" practiced by Erving Goffman[21] was grounded in the recognition that the social setting controls or "frames" how people relate to one another. We adopt "masks" or "personae," not to hide, but rather to let the action in which we are involved come to its "intended" conclusion. People are personally present as actors within the social frame, and irrelevant aspects of the self, the interposition of which might otherwise impede the action, are reserved. In other words, even in utopia, people will still have to relate to one another from time to time as doctor and carpenter and waiter--and perhaps as "sexual actor."[22] Indeed, I would submit that, even in sex within intimacy, an erotic scenario involves the presentation of the self in terms of a "sexual persona." Otherwise the "frame" by which erotic reality[23] is established is not definitively set or is otherwise dissolved. If such is the case, then the conventions of the bar scene are not necessarily depersonalizing; instead, they allow the seduction to reach its appropriate climax and the goods of sex be actualized. The other person is, for the moment, not an individual who is appreciated in the fullness of his individuality, but is rather a "concrete universal,"[24] a *unique* person who has been able to galvanize another's attention on his unique attractive, impressive maleness, and thereby also becomes for that other the momentary focal representative of maleness and of other males. Since the other is both individual and representative, we can understand why he must be experienced as thoroughgoingly masculine, for he must be as impressively male as is necessary for him to attain representative status. Indeed, I will be arguing that tricking is not merely an interaction between two embodied persons, but an interaction whereby each comes into touch with his own masculine maleness through the mediation of a representatively male other.

It might be argued that, to the degree I discover the magnificence of the other in his maleness, I sense myself as deficient in those very respects. That is, the other's attractiveness might seem to depend upon the degree to which I feel myself unattractive. However, a man's ability to get and sustain an erection is directly related to his sense of his own attractiveness. He cannot "perform" if he thinks the other will find him unattractive. Sexual desire is fired not merely by the depth of one's attraction to the other, but by the interplay of one's attraction to the other and the other's attraction to one. Sexual desire--to adapt an image of Gabriel Marcel for our own purposes--"extends a kind of credit"[25] to the other in the expectation that he will prove, in his mysterious otherness, to be someone "for me." Negatively put, sexual desire posits a basic friendliness in the other so that one senses that he will be safe from ridicule and shame as he "uncovers" himself to the gaze and touch of the other.[26] Positively put, arousal depends upon an anticipation of approval and affirmation. In context, this would mean, first, that I sense that my prospective sex partner will be interested in what I expose to his view and manipulation and, secondly, that his pleasure will not be purchased at the expense of mine, but will instead be fueled by my taking pleasure in his taking pleasure in me. The male who is discovered to be unfriendly in the sense used here, no matter how masculinely honed, will find his attractiveness compromised. Friendly responsiveness is finally, to gay desire, an aspect of masculine presence.

I have delayed speaking of anything other than visual and verbal interaction between our two men at the bar until this point. But the tactile sense has been alive all the time. From the moment that a welcome gaze is met and a man knows he is being beheld and watched, a "quickening " of the skin takes place. To become aware of one's gestures through the gaze of the other is to become aware of muscular control and of the stretch and pull of muscle and skin. It is as if the eyes of the other had touched the skin and heralded the touch that might come. But it is in the course of conversation that the first actual touch will occur. Not all touchings are specifically erotic. Shaking hands, and even putting the hand on, or the arm around, another man's shoulder are acts of everyday life. A gesture becomes erotic because of the unusualness of either its placement or timing. A hand on a shoulder may stay there a bit "too" long, or it may begin to caress the neck just below the ear, or even fall to the thigh. Or perhaps a knee, never an organ of touch in everyday commerce, comes to lean on the inside of the other's thigh. In part, it is the unfamiliar feel of the touch that charges it with power. And the unusual, even though expected, takes us, as it were, by surprise. We may first react by a general tightening whose effect is to secure our ordinary sense of ourselves that localizes the self in our heads, all other senses but the visual and the oral being dulled. That is to say, we react defensively. In time, we may melt--or from the onset of the touch, we may give ourselves over to it and "let it be." And, when that happens, what is begun is a relinquishing of ordinary, everyday patterns of consciousness.[27]

The nerves of the body are functioning at all times, and many of the muscles are in contraction in order to sustain the upright posture in and from which most of us engage the world. But we tend not to be aware of such things. Our attentiveness is focused outward upon the world, principally through sight and sound. A twinge might call attention to a muscle--but awareness of a muscle is ordinarily an intrusion, a disruption, of the smooth operation of everyday perception. In ordinary awareness, the body is recessive and is not an explicit object of attention. The body calls attention to itself at the expense of our attentiveness to the world. Our ordinary perceptual attentiveness, moreover, seems to be focused in our head, the center from which we look out upon the world. As it were, we are a perspective on the world from a point which is itself excluded from the field of attention but is usually localized in our head: We can look at our hands and feet, but not at our heads without a mirror. Let us imagine, however, that we are coming home to our house or apartment. Upon unlocking the door, we reach for the light switch only to discover that the light has burned out. If there is no moonlight, street light, or hall light, we are enveloped in darkness. Suppose, further, that our roommate told us that very morning that he or she had planned to rearrange the furniture. What can we say of our consciousness now. We discover as we carefully place our feet, and seek to follow where we are by tracing our fingers on the wall, that we are no longer centered in our head, but in our feet and our fingers. Consciousness has the form of attentiveness, but the place from which we are attentive to the world changes. Consciousness is mobile.

The point of the above excursion is to understand that, to the extent we do not react defensively to, but rather welcome, the prospective sex partner's touch, we have begun to "de-center" our consciousness and localize it diffusely in the skin--with a relative concentration at the place of touch. Since we are still engaged in conversation, speaking and listening, we do not cease to be principally centered in the head. But if we stop talking and close our eyes just to "savor" the moment, we have more or less abdicated head-centered selfhood for a sense of self that is diffused on the surface of the body and is tactilely sensitive. Even now, it will be this diffusion of head-centered consciousness that allows for, and issues in, an incipient erection as a sign of pleasure. What is important to note is that erection comes about through a certain relaxation. Willing an erection to happen--trying to remain centered in the head--is the most reliable way of insuring impotence. Finally, one of the two pulls back from the reverie of tactile delight and recovers sufficient normal functioning to say, "Let's get out of here. Your place or mine?" And the other answers, "Yeah!"

c. At Home Together

The ride home invariably constitutes an intrusion of the ordinary. But after arrival home, and perhaps after a drink, the couple will eventually begin to disrobe, or begin to take each other's clothes off. Disrobing before a relative stranger is itself unnerving (the sense of safety has after all been grounded in "credit") and being undressed by another is highly unusual for an adult--in either case, then, the experience is unnerving and sufficiently dislocates the hold of the ordinary to allow the couple to pick up where they left off--once again beginning to relinquish everyday consciousness to consciousness of tactile pleasure which, in turn, triggers the involuntary--an erection. Although we may speak of the desirability of the "de-genitalization" of sex, it remains a fact that an erect male wants his erection touched. If a hand is near the area, a man will tend to move so that the hand will at least brush the erect phallus. If a head is near by, he may pull the head near as he thrusts his hips forward. And if his partner does not touch his erection, he will touch it himself. (Indeed, I will argue below that "de-genitalization" is but a way of intensifying genitalization!) His partner, now alert to his growing hardness, will himself become intrigued and want to touch what is now so unusually close. In everyday life, another's penis--not to mention an erect one--is usually hidden from public sight. In part because of its very hiddenness, and in part because what is hidden belongs to a stranger, what is usually forbidden and private, a *mysterium fascinans*, is now not only accessible, but solicits touch. Now the partner wants to see and touch what "wants and demands" to be seen and caressed. And as a man indulges his urge to see and touch the other's erection, a child replaces the man. To watch a child with a new object is to begin to see the adult human making love. The infant will caress it, turn it in all sorts of ways to see it from all sides, put it in its mouth, or perhaps see where else it might be able to go. I cannot, however, overestimate the profundity of the experience of finally having gained access to the forbidden--that generally forbidden because it is "private" and because "males don't touch each other that way--ever!" And not merely has one gained access, but the indulgence of one's interest is *welcomed*. And, in testimony to one's mounting sexual desire and to the pleasure of exploring and probing the other freely, one answers with an erection of one's own, an erection which is the gift of worship of solicited desire.

I do not mean to take inventory of the kinds of things gay men do with each other's parts. We can note, however, that the encounter will tend to flow from hand-genital contact, to mouth-genital contact, to penetration of the genital region by the genital--but it need not. The climax of the encounter may be reached with any of the modes of intercourse--the rhythmic caress of the penis by mouth, hand, or ass. Within this general flow, moreover, is to be discerned a rhythm of "titillation." Genital contact will alternate with non-genital contact, and each non-genital contact will enhance the interest in genital contact, until the rhythm of titillation is wholly replaced by the rhythm of penile intercourse. Indeed, the more practiced the lover, the more adroit and innovative he will be with the modes of non-genital contact (as well as innovative in positioning for intercourse). For the practiced lover, even the application of an otherwise intrusive condom can be an instrument of erotic titillation. I have spoken of cruising as a seduction of the self into the body, seducing the self to relinquish "head consciousness" for incarnate, tactile--let us say "body"--consciousness. The rhythm of physical intimacy here serves to ever more thoroughly center the self in and on the genital.

What people do with their eyes and how they speak to one another as they have sex both express and facilitate this unselfconscious focusing of the self as sensitivity to and in the erect phallus. Let us consider first the eyes. A man who is sucking on another will usually, and the man being sucked may, close his eyes. We may say they are "giving themselves up" to the pleasure of the moment. But what is this "giving up"? Just as we may close our eyes if someone asks us to "see" if we can hear what he hears in the street outside the apartment, we do so as a way of "hearing" intently. So, too, our fellated and fellator may close their eyes so as to feel more intently. Indeed, the further into the sexual encounter our men proceed, the more thoroughly they relinquish "head-centered" consciousness as they enjoy the sensations of touch and lick that the other is enjoying indulging them with. Their ordinary sense of self is further destabilized by the unusualness of what is to be felt--tongues not only on genitals or genitals in the mouth, but tongues on armpits, hair nuzzling at the base of the scrotum--and as they find the unusualness of the contact pleasurable, they stretch and contort themselves to invite more--all the time becoming ever more deeply body, rather than "head," consciousness. And all the while they are stimulating one another in surprising places and ways, the genitals assert the demand for further attention by hand or mouth or some other contact.

Suppose a fellator opens his eyes. With the other's cock in his mouth, his eyes behold the expanse of abdomen which stretches across the hips and between pubis and navel. The vistas, being extraordinary, tend to inhibit the return to an everyday "head consciousness"--even as he uses his eyes. That is to say, the eyes become the complement and perhaps extension of tactile contact. But suppose our fellator looks up at the other's face as he continues to suck on him. One who is fucking another anally might also try to watch his fuckee's face. What each is watching for is the effect his actions are having on the other. The fellator or the fucker has returned sufficiently to head-consciousness to assess the other's pleasure. One of the standing features of erotic encounter in all its stages is the degree to which the desire of each is enflamed by the interest in or pleasure the other derives from one's own interest and pleasure. Tony, who always had the "hots" for Darryl, now is enflamed to notice that Darryl seems to have the hots for him even as Darryl is enflamed to know that Tony is being further enflamed by him. At this point, however, we are ready to extrapolate a principle: The best sex is sex in which each derives an equally intense pleasure from the other doing what feels best to him, when each enjoys what the other enjoys doing or being done to him.[28] To see another taking pleasure from my sucking or thrusting is to find myself even more intensely invested in the action in which I may be involved, which is to experience myself as localized more than ever at the places of pleasurable contact.

d. Dirty Talk

Although not all gay men talk when they have sex, attention to what typically comprises "talking dirty" is helpful in this context. To be sure, the most frequently used word among English-speaking gays during sex is "Yeah!" It will most frequently be spoken moaningly, with the vowel sounds held. As such it is a signal of pleasure and by extension an encouragement of the other to do whatever he is doing. A different form of encouragement--almost a "coaching"--can be heard in such words as, "Yeah, you really like that dick, I can tell. Yeah, go down on it. Go all the way down on it." What I think is to be heard here is the attempt of the fellated to facilitate the wholesale investment of the fellator and the fellator's consciousness in the act of sucking. The fellated then finds himself even more thoroughly involved in and through the sensations of his penis. Two other kinds of statements are analogous. In the one, a man encourages his partner to "suck that dick" or perhaps "move that ass." Note in each case, the language speaks of "that" dick or "that" ass, not in terms of "yours" or "mine." Since the language is de-personalized, again it would seem to me a way of dislocating the ordinary sensibility which interprets things in terms of personal possession so as to facilitate the experience of self as fully vested in the pleasurable contact, literally un-self-consciously. So, too, are we to understand such statements as the following: "Open that ass, boy. Let me feel that pussy swallow my dick. Yeah, baby--let me see you take it like a man." As it is, the sequence of thought entails a dizzying mix of metaphors, not to mention a confusion of gender. We might be tempted to see here a series of intended insults: Indeed, the one who is about to be penetrated is serially ... "You boy, you. You woman, you. A man who takes it up the ass!" But the meaning of the words lies less in the clustering of insulting attribution than in the illocutionary force of the entire sequence. In each appellation, the penetrated is called what he is not, for he is neither boy nor woman. But before he has had time to sense the fit or misfit of the name, another totally different attribution is being made. Cumulatively, he is not being allowed to think of himself in terms of any of the names he is being called. The force of the language thus tends to render this kind of "dirty talk" an instrument for dislocating the sense of normal selfhood so as to facilitate what I have come to call "body consciousness."

Sometimes the one who is the penetrator of the moment--after all, such roles are frequently exchanged--will ask, "You like that cock don't you? You like sucking on it, don't you?" or "You like that big cock up your ass, don't you? Tell me how much you like it." For a feminist inspired critic of masculinity such as Stoltenberg,[29] strategic domination is here writ large. The top not only dominates the other--to be top is to be "over" someone else--but he completes the subjugation of the other by making him pretend and/or tell his top that he "likes" his subordination. Preston, however, seems closer to the mark. In his presentation of (S/M) sex in public arenas such as the now defunct Mineshaft,[30] he points out how important it is for the "bottom" to own up to his willingness to endure his passion and, in general, to own up to his desire publicly. In the context of a public arena, Preston argues, even such an elemental homosexual act as cocksucking becomes an occasion to identify and own up to one's desire in the presence of others, letting one's desire become visible to their gaze:[31]

> A player is "man enough" to suck cock in public. He doesn't hide his proclivity. He doesn't claim to be other than his real self. He invites the audience to watch him as he gets on his knees in front of another man dressed in the attire of overt masculinity: the leather of the biker, the uniform of the military man, the outfit of the athlete, all of them garb of this community's expression of masculinity.

By analogy, then, the language of the momentary top in our (vanilla) one-on-one private encounter should be understood as a solicitation for the momentary bottom to own his desire and enjoyment by declaring them to his partner. The partner, in turn, now experiences an even deeper enjoyment as he senses that the other is really delighting in his body and drawing pleasure from the actions which are so pleasurable to him. And again, the "hottest" sex is that sex in which each enjoys the other's indulgence of his individual desires.

Other "dirty" language can be trusted as a key to the psychic transactions in the act of intercourse (or by extension, fellatio to orgasm). Consider the penetrated one, the "bottom," who moans, "Yeah! Oh yeah! Fuck my hot ass." He encourages penetrator, his "top," by communicating his pleasure and thereby invites his top to give himself over even more thoroughly to the act of thrusting, and to experience himself in the pleasure of contact. But where is the bottom's consciousness focused, and on what? If we follow the logic of the argument, he too has now sacrificed head consciousness to body consciousness (shall we say, incarnate consciousness?) and now principally knows pleasure in and through the motion of the other in his rectum. As he comes more and more to be focused in his ass, he is ever more transparently aware of the act of fucking itself until he is finally wholly subsumed by it. Thus carried away by and in the act of fucking, he has ceased to be aware so much of his ass as the source of his pleasure as the cock which is rhythmically penetrating him in a way that he finds so pleasurable. While the power of the thrusting remains alien and beyond him, he is so identified with the act of fucking that the action of the other remains both the other's and vicariously his, and the other's cock becomes for a moment his as well as his top's. "Fuck me!" is not only a challenge to the other not to stop, but also bespeaks the "bottom's" total absorption in the act which is now his as well as his top's. To the extent he senses the top's thrusting as his own it would seem that he has made the maleness of his top his own. But perhaps it is more precise to say that the bottom experiences himself so thoroughly as "the act of fucking" that it is maleness in act (*i.e.*, the joint action of top and bottom) which he experiences as himself.

I am not certain that the "ecstasy" of the top is the same. Indeed, I think there is a fundamental asymmetry in the top's and bottom's experience. While both experience a destabilization of ordinary consciousness and are seduced each by the other into experiencing themselves as totally caught up in and as the rhythmic thrusting of cock, nevertheless the erect phallus which is the focus of attention still belongs to the top as part of his body. The top is focused in "his" cock--while the bottom is focused vicariously on the same cock, this being true whether the top is the source of thrusting, or the bottom, straddling the top, is the source of movement. This "asymmetry" becomes clearer as orgasm approaches. As orgasm nears, vision blurs. If the eyes are open, they become fixed. The hearing is de-sensitized. The oral and the aural cease to be meaningful ways by which a man experiences himself in the world. Moreover, he feels himself carried along by what is in fact an autonomous rhythm. He has been seduced into giving up ordinary consciousness until he is now in the grip of the uncontrollable rhythm of penile thrust and withdrawal until that is in turn succeeded by the spasmodic rhythm of ejaculation. Both top and bottom experience themselves for the moment totally and unreservedly as "cock"--and thereby experience themselves as fully male. I am not arguing that "being a man" is the same as "being a cock," but rather that the experience of self in, through, and as cock is to come to experience the self as vitally male. I am making a point not unrelated to Gaylin's when he writes, "Anything that reduces a man in any field can also make him *feel* sexually impotent, powerless at this seminal level. Reciprocally, any signs of sexual impotence will diminish his sense of power among other men in the competitive worlds beyond sexuality."[32] In contrast to Gaylin's negative formulations, I make the positive claim that, sensing himself in, through, and as potent cock during sex, a man is empowered to feel himself and to be a man in the world beyond sex.

We had begun to explore a possible asymmetry between the bottom's and the top's experiences. Let us resume that exploration by attending to the postures of each as orgasm approaches. Viewed from the side, the orgasmic top's typical posture will resemble a question mark: the torso is rounded forward so that the head is drawn down, as if looking at the crotch, and the legs are stretched pushing upward so as to thrust the hips in the direction of the face. The posture cannot help but focus the whole experience of self in the protruding, now ejaculating cock. If the bottom has not reached orgasm by the time the top has, it is conventional that the top leaves his cock in his bottom as long as possible. If detumescence has caused him to "fall out," he will usually continue to manipulate the bottom's anus with the hand to sustain the illusion that the bottom is still being fucked. Typically, then, the hips of the bottom will not be thrust forward even as orgasm approaches, but rather he will push downward and back into his top's crotch even as his legs are in "squat" position. When a man ejaculates, the sphincter muscle contracts. For the top, this contraction is experienced as part of the total muscular contraction of forward thrust. For the bottom, however, the sphincter contracts around something. Up until the point of orgasm, he has experienced himself primarily as sensitivity to the other's thrusting cock. His own cock now comes into more focal significance as orgasm approaches. While orgasm is still a matter of penile ejaculation, what he experiences as "cock" will comprehend what he has "incorporated" anally. The top, as it were, comes into the fullness of his maleness with the bottom as his adoring "mirror," a masculine male whose "gaze" can and does confirm the maleness that he feels he is by virtue of his orgasmic identification with his own cock. The bottom likewise experiences himself as fully male by virtue of his own cock, but his own cock is experienced as rooted in and continuous with the cock of his impressively male other. While the top feels himself male and is confirmed as such by the bottom, the bottom experiences himself in an "augmented" maleness--all the while "encouraged" to do so by his fellow male. I repeat, there is certainly more to being a man than being a cock. But I do claim that experiencing the self as cock in the act of sex, welcomed as that experience is by another man, is a way, if not the way, by which gay men can--and do--come to experience themselves as fully and vitally male. To sense the self as cock is to be empowered as a man in the world. The cock is not the man, nor the man the cock. But the cock is the sign, symbol, and--above all in this context--the vehicle, I will argue, of masculine identity and empowerment.

We have one more feature of the encounter to note before we finish this part of the analysis. It is to be noted that the human male responds to the approaching orgasm of another with a physiological empathy. He will begin to breathe hard with the pronounced rhythmic breathing of the one reaching orgasm--and tend to feel stirrings in the genitalia even if they have just ejaculated, as if building to another. And he may feel compelled to hold the other tightly. In accordance with the principle of reciprocity we have seen at work throughout the encounter, whereby the desire and pleasure of the other fires the self's desire for the other, so such "empathetic cumming" serves to reinforce the intensity of each other's orgasm when orgasm is mutual. Usually, each attains to orgasm separately, but in the company of the other, encouraged by the sympathetic response. Whatever the scenario--whether orgasm is mutual or successive--the sense that one has been "seduced" into incarnating oneself in a body consciousness that ultimately led to orgasm is inescapable--that the whole experience has been facilitated by the other. One has become un-self-consciously body in the arms of another man, another male body, indeed one who has seemed to one impressively male.

3. Conclusions

Our attempt at a phenomenological analysis of tricking has now been completed. It is time to try to outline the perspective that has emerged. I have argued that the ecstasy of sex is not specifically a self-transcending experience, but an experience in which one is "seduced," that is, facilitated by another, into experiencing another way of living the body. Sex is a matter of attaining to incarnate sensitivity; that is, a mode of consciousness in which one's interaction with the world is above all in and through the tactile. It involves a relaxation of head-consciousness to the point that the self is subsumed by the autonomous. To some, it is this experience of being carried away that is determinative and may even be interpreted as a union with some putative ontological reality. Rather, it seems to me, tricking, as I have portrayed it, cries out to be understood, on the one hand, on the analogy of a ritual of initiation, with both an intra-psychic and a social dimension, and on the other, as an important interpersonal experience.

a. To Be A Man

In its conventionality, tricking can be seen as a form of ritual behavior. In societies which have male initiation ceremonies, such ceremony is the symbol and vehicle of a boy's entrance into manhood. Once having undergone the ceremony, the boy comes to thinks of himself--as do others --as an adult male and he can now join the company of men. It functions to secure an identity and to incorporate the boy into the male body politic. Tricking, it seems to me, functions in a similar way.[33] By whichever path, the way of the top or the way of the bottom, sexual engagement is a way of experiencing the self as impressively, masculinely male. Each is assisted by an impressively male other to experience himself as fully, impressively male, the bottom vicariously and the top integrally. Such an experience is not for the moment alone, but is an invitation to center the sense of self in this new sense of being male, a sense of being fully male despite whatever sense of inadequacy may haunt us. To the extent that such a sense of self has become established, the repetition of the experience becomes a celebratory rite of recognition, of re-cognition.

To be totally centered as sensitivity to and in the cock--to experience oneself un-self-consciously as cock, as wholly subsumed in maleness--is, in the first place, an occasion to experience the self freed from the power of the comparatives that ordinarily control our experience. A man who suffers from a sense of being short is, for the moment, delivered from a sense that he is short; the man who is self-conscious about the size of his penis is delivered for the moment from his sense of inadequacy; the older man is no longer old; and the thin man and the fat man for the moment are neither thin nor fat. Cumming, we come into our own as male bodies in the world, rooted in the world as such.

Sex, then, mediates a sense of being alive vitally as a male, a sense of virility. But what is at stake for gay men is not merely a way of feeling the self, but also a way of thinking about the self. At stake in sex is not merely virility, but masculinity. Gay men in America grow up in a culture which is overwhelmingly dominated by the "heterosexual ideal." Men are expected not only to desire women, but to desire women exclusively. That is to say, a man not only desires women, but he does not desire other men. In our culture, then, a man who experiences homoerotic desire for another man cannot help but experience such desire as a compromise of his masculinity. I want to argue that the experience of gay sex facilitates a resolution of such cognitive dissonance in favor of the masculine. In sex, a gay man comes to know himself as fundamentally, if deviantly, masculine. Each sex partner has been attracted by the masculinity of the other, and each is confirmed in and through the interaction with the other as masculine. And the discovery of the self as masculine represents a transformed--perhaps, revolutionary--understanding of masculinity.

In our culture, there is an interrelation in the rhetoric of sex and of gender. We can "have sex" as either the penetrator or the penetrated, the "fucker" or the "fuckee." But the phrase "to fuck" ordinarily connotes the action of penetration, as in "I want to fuck her" or "He fucked me." The male, the possessor of the phallus, the instrument of penetration, then is identified as the actor in the drama. The male, then, becomes the penetrator. As the penetrator, he is the "active" agent; and the receptive partner is the "passive" one. "Masculinity," in turn, becomes defined in terms of penetration: Masculinity inheres in penetrating, not in being penetrated; and a "real" man comes to be understood as one who can penetrate, but cannot be penetrated. Men are ideally impenetrable penetrators.

Bernadette Brooten has spoken of alternative ways of construing the act of sex: "For example, one could conceptualize the woman swallowing the male penis--enfolding, encircling, embracing, or otherwise taking in the penis."[34] Such alternative rhetorical strategies would certainly undermine the usual attribution of activity and passivity in sex. However, it is not the rhetoric of sex that concerns me here, but rather the idea of "masculinity." If, in gay sex, our so-called "top" is confirmed in his masculinity because of the admiring gaze of a masculine yet penetrable man, and if our so-called "bottom" can experience himself as masculine even if penetrated by another, then masculinity comes to transcend the act of penetration, and penetrability becomes an admissible part of masculine behavior and sensibility. Gays thus, I would suggest, win through to a revolutionary concept of masculinity important to the growing "crisis" of masculinity in our time.[35]

b. To Be A Man Among Men

Sex, I have argued, is an affair with one who seems to us impressively male which allows one to feel and know oneself overwhelmingly in one's maleness, one's virility and one's masculinity. But it is not merely the case that I discover myself through sex, but that I come into my own in the arms of another man who has welcomed and encouraged my "incarnation." As "impressively male," he is also a representative of other men. The worlds we inhabit in everyday life do not always "welcome" us, but in the sexual encounter I am confronted with a representative of the whole who has been "for me" in the ways traced above. I discover the world of men "proleptically;" as it were, in an "anticipatory attainment"[36] of what is, can, and ought to be. In Christian tradition, the Eucharist is both a meal in which the community bodies forth what it essentially is, a "family" of companions, and is at the same time a symbol of the messianic banquet and indeed of the entire "world to come." So too, then, sex is a sacrament, but a sacrament of what? Kevin Gordon has isolated "fraternal friendship"[37] as the model for ethical wisdom "emerging from the communal experience of its own moral geography." Richard Mohr has argued a case for seeing gay sexual reality in particular, in its ideal dimension, as democratic.[38] My analysis would lend support to Mohr's formulation. Ideal sex, I am arguing, derives from a delight of each in each other's doing what each wants to do. Sexual experience thus provides an experiential model for an assent to, if not delight in, each living the life that he sees he wants insofar as it is possible and not unethical.[39] Perhaps we are not far off the mark by speaking of a democratic conviviality.

c. Meeting, Intimacy, and the Rule of Friendship

But tricking is at the same time an affair between two individuals, each of whom is "fraught with background."[40] Simply put, the sexual encounter is a way of getting to know another as person in the fullness of his personhood. I quote Richard Mohr again:[41]

> ... from the way a person presents and bears his body to you, from the way he touches and attends your body, you learn immediately what the person's values are; one learns whether his concerns extend beyond himself, whether he is patient, whether he is inventive, whether he is attentive and caring or whether he is inventive and self-centered, whether he can rise above social expectation, and, importantly, whether he respects himself.

For gay men, then, casual sex is above all a ritual greeting and meeting. To the extent that we tend to like whoever gives us pleasure, we might understand casual sex as having a dynamism which predisposes each to be with--and, therefore, to get to know[42]--the other more. But the fact of the matter is that we may have found that the fellow is not one who is to our liking and we may decide, quite legitimately, that we do not wish to interact with him further. Or it might happen that we discover that another is truly an interesting person, but for whatever reason, we cannot or do not want a relationship, in which case, not to cultivate further interrelations might also be legitimate. But if our partner wants further contact because he wants or might want a more or less "long-term" lover and, having been auditioning us for the part, it behooves us to develop the art of friendly rebuff. Not tricking,[43] but how we treat our tricks, is the truly legitimate locus of ethical consideration. And I would argue that, in principle, we should not act in such a way as to compromise that basic friendliness to which the act of sex introduces and reintroduces us. Tricking would be equivalent to ethical abuse only if it involved such exploitation as[44]

> ... taking advantage of another's limited alternatives, desperate situation, or dire needs; manipulating another into consent through use of an inequality of power; ... [or] undermining the voluntary or informed consent of another through deception or various forms of physical or economic coercion.

In the present context, such exploitation would be in violation of the spirit of democratic friendship which the sexual experience reveals sacramentally. Barring such, "trick sex," as I have shown it, is structured by a mutual "treasuring." Moreover, "trick sex" would be ethically problematic if tricking involved the violation of a pact of monogamous sexual constancy made with a third party.

While sex need not be, it *can be* an expression of intimacy between intimates as well as a symbol for intimacy. What is intimacy? In part it is the space between friends in which each can bare the self in many ways to the other and not experience abandonment by the other. To the extent that revealing the self can be imaged as a baring of the "private," the "baring of the private parts" can be a symbol for such self-revelation. Sexual affirmation can be the symbol for that friend's interest that keeps him there and prohibits the very thought of abandoning the other. Thus, sex is a symbol. But it can also express that enduring interest to the extent that familiarity with the other does not compromise his sexiness. Indeed, good sex between intimates is difficult--else there would not be so much press, especially in the straight world, about keeping the marriage alive or keeping the sex in the relation. Sex between intimates must chart its course between the Scylla of a familiarity (knowing too much about the other that compromises his sexiness) and the Charybdis of trivialization (having such easy access to the other's bodily privates that they seem to loose their impressiveness). So Russell Vannoy[45] would write a philosophy of sex which argues for the ethical legitimacy of sex without any reference to "love" and asserts its experiential preeminence: Sex with a stranger is just plain "hotter" sex. And gay couples will experiment with a variety of forms of open marriage[46]--so much do they value hot sex and so rarely do they find relational sex hot. Those for whom loving sex is still hot are truly among the blessed. But because they are blessed, others are simply less blessed or even unlucky, not for that reason immoral or even immature.

* * *

As I bring this series of reflections to a close, I cannot but notice how much more would need to be said in a full phenomenology of sex. Above all, one would have to attend more fully to those things that trigger sexual desire. One would have to attend to whatever fantasies of nurturance at the breast and of cannibalism, for example, that might very well be a source for the relish with which we throw ourselves into sex. A full accounting of the meaning of sex would have to take such fantasies into account as well. At the same time, I know full well that phenomenology fails as a science. Its public verifiability lies in the responsive chords it rouses in others, whether they recognize their experience in and through the account. What I hope is that I have given an account which is sufficiently true to sever the equation of treating another as a sexual object with abuse and to establish a recognition of the validity that casual sex can have in the life of a gay man as a vehicle of his "humanization"--a process which some of us recognize as the substance of spirituality. Some might be tempted to argue that sex figures too highly in the lives of gay men, that they are more concerned with being desirable than with being, shall we say, successful.[47] But the male ego is cunning. As we have already noted above, a sense of deficiency in power in the world of everyday business is frequently sufficient to render a man impotent in bed.[48] But so too can his power in the world be emboldened by the solidity in being he finds in bed. I hope in some way to have made plausible Paul Goodman's hunch that "homosexual promiscuity enriches more lives than it desensitizes."[49]

---

[1]See, in particular, Martin P. Levine, "The Life and Death of Gay Clones" in Gilbert Herdt, *Gay Culture in America: Essays from the Field* (Boston: Beacon Press, 1992), p.75. The idea is echoed in a number of essays in that book.

[2]We are, at the very beginning of this study, faced with a terminological difficulty. Contemporary English seems to lack an appropriate word or phrase to indicate exactly the kind of sex which many gay men (especially in the urban ghettos) have. Too many semantic candidates turn out to be misnomers. Gay sex is so far from casual that "casual" or "recreational sex" are ruled out. The fact that one frequently knows the name (if very little else) of one's sexual partner rules out the phrase "anonymous sex" to categorize the whole class of encounters. "Promiscuous sex" implies a lack of discrimination which simply does not ring true--it matters to us who touches us sexually. And no sexual encounter is literally "non-relational." I am left with the colloquial "fucking around" or the awkward "sex outside of an intimate relation." Perhaps the coinage "trick sex" is least misleading, less "impolite," and minimally awkward.

[3]Frank Browning, *The Culture of Desire: Paradox and Perversity in Gay Lives Today* (New York: Crown Publishers, Inc., 1993), pp. 80f.

[4]*Ibid.*, p. 81.

[5]Diotima, the instructor of Socrates in Plato's *Symposium*, first represents sexual desire to be the most privileged example through which one can discern the intentionality--to use modern jargon--of all human *eros*. But, once having isolated immortal happiness as the "real" object of human erotic desiring, sexual desire is relegated to being a particularly misguided way of trying to attain the real object of the heart's desire. Augustine would take the next step of calling sexual desire a form of "lust" with the result that even sex within marriage would seem to him but "licit lust." While drawing upon the Buddhist and Christian traditions repectively, Richard Wagner follows the example of Gottfried von Strassburg in portraying the relation between Tristan and Isolde by means of religious imagery. It is interesting to note that, in Wagner's opera, sex enters the picture only in and through the rhythmic and chromatic movement of the *Liebestode*, thus rendering sex but a symbol for that real merger of selves that the lovers long for but can have only in death. Platonic and romantic eros are both essentially de-sexualized.

[6]Andre Guindon, *The Sexual Creators: An Ethical Proposal for Concerned Christians* (Lanham, MD: University of America, 1986), *passim.*

[7]Carter Heyward, *Touching Our Strength: The Erotic as Power and the Love of God* (San Francisco: Harper and Row, 1989), esp. p. 135.

[8]Mary E. Hunt, *Fierce Tenderness: A Feminist Theology of Friendship* (New York: Crossroad, 1991), e.g. p. 3.

[9]J. Michael Clark with Bob McNeir, *Masculine Socialization & Gay Liberation: A Conversation on the Work of James Nelson & Other Wise Friends* (Arlington, TX: The Liberal Press, 1992), p. 7-8. It is salient that Clark refers to himself in the text as a "male lesbian" indicating the extent to which his opinions are at variance with what he understands as typically gay (p. 13).

[10]Michael Callen, "Come One, Come All!" *QW* (May 10, 1992), p. 59.

[11]In part, the essay that follows is one small attempt to answer the challenge that Kevin Gordon issued for the gay community to

bring to consciousness what it knows of sex. *Cf.* Kevin Gordon, "The Sexual Bankruptcy of the Christian Traditions: A Perspective of Radical Suspicion and of Fundamental Trust" in David G. Hallman, ed., *AIDS Issues: Confronting the Challenge* (New York: The Pilgrim Press, 1989), p. 209.

[12]Let me be clear that, in using the term "spiritual," I do not mean "the mystical" (whatever that may mean) or imply any notion of God-relation, as the term usually does in Western religious discourse. Rather I think of spirituality as a person's (or perhaps a group's) basic sense of self and vocation, the way he or she might steady his or her course, and the tone and style of his or her life.

[13]Clark is particularly prone to think in such "either/or" categories when it comes to sex. *Cf.*: "Just going out for sex is very dehumanizing; it doesn't deal with people as people, it treats people only as sex objects." Clark, *Masculine Socialization,* p. 10.

[14]Judith Butler, *Gender Trouble: Feminism and the Subversion of Identity* (New York: Routledge, 1990), pp. 134-141. Butler's characterization of drag parody suggests a wholly contingent relation between sex, gender identification, and gender performance that I would question. However, in understanding masculine gender as "effect," it readily becomes apparent why one's masculinity *needs* confirmation from significant masculine others.

[15]Richard D. Mohr, *Gay Ideas: Outing and Other Controversies* (Boston: Beacon Press, 1992), p. 163.

[16]This leaves open the question of what kind of male embodiedness constitutes the definitively male in a given situation and how differences in this regard are to be accounted for. Contemporary gay iconography suggests the preference for the youthful (usually smooth-bodied) Apollonian athletic type over the maturer (sometimes hirsute) Herculean type. The threat of AIDS might cause the look of innocence (ideally non-threatening because inexperienced) to acquire a certain appeal. A possible sex-partner, I will argue, must not pose any ultimate threat. But other factors are surely ingredient here, a topic which I take up in "An Affair of Men: Masculinity and the Dynamics of Gay Sex," *The Journal of Men's Studies* 3.1 (August 1994).

[17]To be distinguished from the comments, "He's a real girl!" which translates, "He may be slightly effeminate, but he's a nice guy who loves to get fucked."

[18]To be sure, the sexual fascination with the "hunk" reveals a certain erotic privilege, and our egalitarian sensibilities--or our *ressentiment* (Nietzsche should not be forgotten here)--may protest that eroticism ought to be more democratic, that people ought to look for more than "just a beautiful body." At any rate, if sexual interest is responsiveness to beauty, then it is inescapable that there will be a privileged elite. However, as I note below, the beauty of a body--its appearance--can be undermined by a man's unfriendliness or unreceptiveness. And I would extend the point to argue that facets of character can either augment or defuse the apparent beauty of a body. Those with a "beautiful" character ultimately begin to look beautiful, while even a person with a beautiful body will begin to appear less beautiful to the degree familiarity makes us aware of the "ugliness" of his character. But, I would insist, it is still the beauty of the body--however transfigured by the beauty or deformity of character--that is the focus of erotic responsiveness. Unfortunately, familiarity can also have a way of undermining the presentational immediacy of sexiness.

[19]Richard D. Mohr uses the language of "privacy." See his *Gays/Justice: A Study of Ethics, Society, and Law* (New York: Columbia University Press, 1988), pp. 100-6. Murray S. Davis speaks of the slippage into "erotic reality." See his *Smut: Erotic Reality/Obscene Ideology* (Chicago: The University of Chicago Press, 1983), pp. 1-86, *passim.*

[20]Mohr, *Gay Ideas,* p. 29.

[21]*Cf.*, for example, Erving Goffman, *The Presentation of the Self in Everyday Life* (Garden City, NY: Doubleday & Co., 1959).

[22]*Cf.* Scott Tucker, "Radical Feminism and Gay Male Porn" in Michael S. Kimmel, ed., *Men Confront Pornography* (New York: Meridian Books, 1991), pp. 264-6.

[23]Davis, *Smut, op cit.*

[24]In his book *Sexual Desire: A Moral Philosophy of the Erotic* (New York: The Free Press, 1986), arguably the most phenomenologically astute and philosophically sophisticated defense of the sex-is-justified-by-intimacy position, Roger Scruton distinguishes between sexual desire and love, yet insists that the other "points" to the latter. His argument turns on the claim that in both sexual desire and love we are focussed on an irreplaceable other person; only loving sex is therefore true to the full intentionality of sexual desire. However, it seems to me that Scruton may be using "person" as the focus of sexual

desire and of love in an equivocal sense. In the gay situation at hand, the focus is on an irreplaceable and unique other person, but not on a person in his density as an existential individual.

[25]Gabriel Marcel, *The Mystery of Being. Vol 2, Faith & Reality*, trans. by Rene Hague (South Bend, IN: Regnery/Gateway, 1979), pp. 77 & 79. *Cf.* the discussion of Marcel on this point in Ronald E. Long, *Keeping Faith With the Dead: An Approach to Religion Through the Writings of Josiah royce, Gabriel Marcel, and George Santayana.* Ph.D. dissertation (Ann Arbor, MI: University Microfilms International, 1985), pp. 103-4.

[26]What the prospect of HIV transmission through sex has brought home to us so vividly in the age of AIDS is that sexual arousal depends upon a sense of safety, not only from shame and ridicule, but from bodily harm. To be aroused by another is to posit that he is no threat to one's life. One cannot become erect in fear. To be sure, there is nothing in life without risk--least of all, an "extension of credit." In actual practice, my "friend" may turn out to be no friend at all. Whom arousal posits and experiences as "friend" is, as it were, a projection in defiance of *actual* risk. And many gay men find the conventions of "safe sex" sufficient warrant to allow one to treat a prospective trick as "friend."

[27]The account of consciousness that follows depends heavily upon the phenomenological analysis of Drew Leder, *The Absent Body* (Chicago: The University of Chicago Press, 1990).

[28]I owe this insight to Dr. Gerald Perlman, Ph.D., in a private communication.

[29]See, for example, John Stoltenberg, *The End of Masculinity: A Book for Men of Conscience* (New York: Dutton, 1993).

[30]John Preston, "The Theater of Sexual Initiation" in John Preston, *My Life As a Pornographer & Other Indecent Acts* (New York: Masqerade Books, 1993), pp. 49-63.

[31]*Ibid.*, p. 60.

[32]Willard Gaylin, *The Male Ego* (New York: Viking, 1993), p. 133.

[33]Both Preston's ("Theater") and Hopcke's analyses make a similar claim for S/M sex. *Cf.* Robert H. Hopcke, "S/M and the psychology of gay male initiation: An archetypal perspective," in Mark Thompson, ed., *Leatherfolk: Radical Sex, People, Politics, and Practice* (Boston: Alyson Publications, 1991), pp. 65-76. In both cases,

the analogy is, of course, limited: initiation is a ceremony, for example, done only once. Yet, because both tricking and ritual initiation consolidate identity and community, I think the analogy is generally valid.

[34]Bernadette Brooten, with Edouard Fontenot, "Of Love Spells and Lesbians in Ancient Rome," *The Harvard Gay and Lesbian Review* Vol. 1, No. 2 (Spring, 1994), p. 11.

[35]Richard D. Mohr has recently argued that the recent controversy over gays in the military was rooted in the symbolism of penetration. A solider is expected to be an impenetrable penetrator. Hence, there is a conceptual difficulty is seeing women and (willingly) penetrable men (gays) as soldiers. Arguing that the military is the medium through which the country defines itself and what citizenship means, Mohr points out that lifting the ban on gays in the military would start us down the road to redefinition of ourselves as a people. To the extent the citizen soldier is a model for what it means to be a full, real person, then the inclusion of gays in the military will allow for a more relaxed, less defensive and more commodious life for us all. See Richard D. Mohr, *A More Perfect Union: Why Straight America Must Stand Up for Gay Rights* (Boston: Beacon Press, 1994), esp. 116-119.

[36]The term derives from the unjustly neglected work of William Ernest Hocking. *Cf.* his *The Meaning of God in Human Experience* (New Haven: Yale University Press, 1963).

[37]Gordon, "Sexual Bankruptcy," pp. 203-204.

[38]Mohr, *Gay Ideas*, esp. pp. 195-201.

[39]*Cf.* how one critic of the work of pornographic artist Tom of Finland describes the world he perceives that work to embody:

> It is the sexiness of the men in the drawings that first impresses the viewer, then the comradery [*sic*] amongst Tom's Men kicks in. Actually their comradery is part of their sexiness and vice versa. Look at the faces. These guys are talking, feeling creatures who like what they are doing. They work hard to get what they want and need. They participate willingly with each other--smiling, laughing, singing, crying, getting nasty, leering, showing off, demanding, submitting, sharing. ...They like themselves; they enjoy each other and they appreciate you, their audience. Everyone is equal. For all that may be said about Tom's drawing promoting casual

sex, Tom's men qualify it as meaningful casual sex--sharing and full of friendship, emotions, challenges, and thoughts.

From Hudson, "Tom of Finland--An Appreciation" in *Tom of Finland: Retrospective II* (Los Angeles: Tom of Finland Foundation, 1991), p. 5. While I think "Hudson's" reading of Tom's drawings is generally correct, it must be noted that Tom also depicts in some of his drawings instances of male rape in which the "delight" of the bottom seems irrelevant.

[40]The term derives from Erich Auerbach, *Mimesis; The Representation of Reality in Western Literature,* trans. by Willard Trask (Garden City,New York: Doubleday Anchor Book, 1957), p. 10.

[41]Mohr, *Gay Ideas*, p. 199.

[42]As Mohr further notes in the same passage, *ibid.*

[43]To be sure, all good things are, in human hands, liable to distortion. Tricking may become morally problematic to the extent that it becomes "addictive." Addictive tricking is distorted because in part it is bad sex--when access to the mysterious privates of another becomes all too familiar, sex is trivializaed. Secondly, the habitual need for new tricks may foreclose on the possibility of capitalizaing of other possibilities such as intimacy, should they be desired. But then, it is not tricking as such, but addictive behavior that is the problem.

[44]Raymond A. Belliotti, "Sex" in Peter Singer, ed., *A Companion to Ethics.* Blackwell Companions to Philosophy Series (Cambridge, MA: Basil Blackwell, 1991), pp. 325f. In this passage, he is arguing that a basically Kantian view of avoiding "using" others as objects needs specificity if it is to qualify as a legitimate norm of ethical discrimination, further stating that even the above ideas need further determination to make them viable. Belliotti has expanded and refined his position in his recently released *Good Sex: Perspectives on Sexual Ethics* (Lawrence, KS: University of Kansas, 1993).

[45]Russell Vannoy, *Sex Without Love: A Philosophical Exploration* (Buffalo: Prometheus Books, 1980).

[46]J. Michael Clark provides a particularly good guide to the emotional difficulties which attend such "open marriages." See his *A Defiant Celebration: Theological Ethics & Gay Sensibility* (Garland, TX: Tangelwueld Press, 1990), esp. pp. 39-50.

[47]*Cf.* Alan Ebert, "To be fat and gay is a contradiction in terms," *Christopher Street* Vol. 1, No. 5 (November, 1976), p. 26. This article is credited as being an excerpt from a book of interviews

that was to be published by Macmillan under the title *The Homosexuals: Who and What We Are.*

[48]See Gaylin, *Male Ego*, p. 133.

[49]Quoted in Mohr, *Gay ideas*, p. 198.

Robin Gorsline & Daniel T. Spencer

Putting Our Bodies on the Line: Markers for Justice

Continuing the Conversation Between Lesbians & Gay Men in Religion

This paper grows out of our discussions about two papers presented at the joint session conducted by the Lesbian-Feminist Issues in Religion Group and the Gay Men's Issues in Religion Group in San Francisco, November 1992: "Opposites Do Not Always Attract: How and Why Lesbian Women and Gay Men Diverge Religiously" by Mary Hunt and "Embodying the Connections: What Lesbians Can Learn from Gay Men about Sex and What Gay Men Must Learn from Lesbians about Justice" by Carter Heyward (printed in volume 5 of this series).

We assume the desirability of effective, continuing coalitions among lesbian women and gay men for justice.[1] However, we recognize the warning signals raised by Heyward's and Hunt's observations about the experiential and locational differences between lesbian women and gay men which contribute to continuing divisions and lack of coherent coalitions rather than solidarity and effective social and ecclesial action. At the same time, we are cognizant of a continuing desire by many lesbian women and gay men to work closely together for justice, work which includes celebrating the life-giving power of our sexualities. At issue, then, is this question: How can lesbian women and gay men work *together* for justice, not only for ourselves but for all the oppressed in our midst.

As white profeminist gay men, we believe this joint work requires careful attention to the multi-layered complexities which mark the enactment of privilege in particular circumstances. We recognize that we, as white, highly educated men, enjoy considerable privilege in our society relative to those who are not white, not male, or neither, and that privilege is often, if not generally, reflected in the structures of power within lesbian and gay communities. Communal work for justice requires not only efforts to overturn such privilege, but also an insistence on accountability for how it is used by the more privileged in the struggle for justice for all.

We offer this paper in order to generate a conversational response that invites more voices into the conversation. After highlighting some of the key points raised in Hunt's and Heyward's papers, we explore some avenues of how differences between lesbians and gay men are reflected in our communities and U.S. society by the ways our bodies function as social markers to signify acceptable boundaries and meanings in wider society. We reflect on the particularities of gay male experiences and suggest some guidelines for gay men--especially white gay men--to shape our ongoing participation with lesbian women and other gay men in the shared praxis of justice and survival.

Mary Hunt argued clearly and forcefully that to accomplish the historical process of inclusion and justice for lesbian, gay and bisexual persons, we must have a clear sense of who we are. Historically we have been treated by the churches and society as an undifferentiated unit. This has functioned to obscure real and important differences that exist between and among us. While unity between lesbian women and gay men often has been our only survival option when faced with the hostility of church and society, it has come at a price: As Hunt stated so cogently, it maintains a facade of "equal opportunity liberation in an unequal world and church" that ignores the different obstacles set up not just by sexuality, but by gender, race, and class as well.

Underlying this false inclusion is a deep lack of mutual understanding of each other's experience and commitments. Gay men in particular have demonstrated little understanding of and solidarity with lesbian women's commitment to issues such as abortion rights, opposing violence against women, pay equity, and anti-racism work. Examining three historical periods of lesbian, gay, and now bisexual thought, Hunt shows how in each lesbian experience and concerns have been subsumed under and collapsed into gay male-centered categories and movements. For this historical moment Hunt believes the time has come to admit and explore our *differences* to sort out our respective *strengths*. If we can do this we may then be able to find our *commonalties* to bolster our respective *weaknesses*.

Carter Heyward's paper does just this in exploring what lesbians and gay men have to offer each other in light of a shared commitment to hold together justice and pleasure. She begins by asking, can sex be good and pleasurable for lesbians (and all women) in a sexually violent and misogynist culture, and what will gay men gain and lose in resisting the dynamics of sexual violence and sexism? Heyward argues that gay men can contribute to lesbians' reclaiming sex as good and pleasurable in itself only when gay men first operate from a profeminist stance committed to the well-being of women. This means connecting our lovemaking to our justicemaking, and examining how men's sexual practices--including those of gay and bisexual men--have been shaped by and contribute to sexist constructions of women. When gay men take justice for women and others seriously, lesbians and gay men can work together to foster a shared primary moral agency: "to help create the yearning and conditions for non-violent, non-abusive life together."

We agree with the analyses and commitments of Hunt and Heyward. We take seriously the implications of our profeminist stance in our theology and praxis, and the need to take responsibility for examining our own histories, analyses, and social privilege in light of being shaped by and participating in hierarchical social relations based on differences of gender, race, and class. However, we not only share Hunt's concern for the inappropriate lumping together of gay men and lesbian women, but also are concerned that gay men not be made to appear as one vast lump of (hetero)male privilege. The complex relations which mark privilege often undercut explanations based on dichotomous categories of gender, race, class or sexual preference. We contend that bodies, lesbian female and gay male bodies, are primary loci for revealing the multiple layers of privilege--both among those with more and those with less privilege. The bodies of lesbian women and gay men often are inscribed as social markers that demarcate social and cultural boundaries both within the lesbian and gay communities and the larger society. Thus, an adequate description and analysis of the relative presence *and* absence of bodily integrity within various segments of our different communities may reveal much about not only the complex operations of privilege but also the possibilities of and requirements for justice.

We cite here five examples of the ways lesbian and gay male bodies are inscribed as social markers that illustrate some of the ways these differences operate. The first three are experiences common across our communities, the latter two are more prevalent in gay male experience. In each case, paying attention to difference and particularity may reveal some of the ways differences in lesbian and gay social locations and experience influence how we interpret the social meaning of these phenomena.

1. Lesbian & gay male bodies & violations of bodily integrity

The violation of our bodily integrity, either self-inflicted under the pressures of homophobia, sexism and/or racism or inflicted by others, is characteristic of both lesbian and gay male experience(s), crossing boundaries of race and class. The sum of the different forms indicates the high price to be paid for trying to integrate one's gay or lesbian identity in a profoundly anti-homoerotic context. Surviving adolescence is the first challenge for many of us. Government sponsored studies reveal that gay and lesbian youth are three times as likely as heterosexual youth to commit suicide and that close to 30% of teenagers who do commit suicide are struggling with issues of homosexuality.[2]

If we survive our teenage years, many of us respond to external and internalized homophobia and other pressures by resorting to destructive and addictive behaviors. Chemical and alcohol abuse run high in our communities; it is estimated that alcoholism and drug addiction among lesbians and gay men is about three times the rate among the general population--one in three versus one in ten.[3] Another experience of the violation of our bodily integrity we hold in common is the threat and reality of anti-gay and anti-lesbian violence. Physical violence and hate crimes against lesbians and gay men continue to escalate. The New York Lesbian and Gay Anti-Violence Project reports that 982 lesbians or gay men were victims of hate crimes in 1992--a doubling of anti-lesbian and anti-gay male violence in the last three years alone.[4] A 1990 survey of 400 lesbians in San Francisco found that two thirds had been assaulted within the previous year. With other surveys showing that upwards of 20% of gay men and lesbians report being victimized by the police, it is not surprising that only 15% of the women in the San Francisco survey reported their assaults to the police.[5]

We are familiar with these and other statistics that demonstrate the difficult challenge of maintaining bodily integrity in our communities. Our bodies are inscribed by society as markers that set limits on embodying alternatives to models of compulsory heterosexuality; our bodies are marked by the high toll exacted from choosing to live with integrity as lesbians and gay men. Yet too rarely do the social and ethical analyses of these epidemics of bodily violence pay close attention to difference in exploring the dynamics that generate them. The article on teen suicide in *The Advocate*, for example, reported almost exclusively on teenage boys, perpetuating the invisibility of teenage lesbians and subsuming the particularity of their experience under the generic (male) category of gay teen suicide. Yet to accurately understand and address lesbian and gay teen suicide, we need to be asking how the dynamics of homophobia intersect with sexism and other pressures differently for girls than for boys in adolescence, and for youth in locations that differ by race and class.

Similarly, while the common link in virtually all cases of anti-lesbian and anti-gay violence is that the perpetrators are straight-identified men, the dynamics often differ. Gay men are bashed for a variety of reasons: for not participating in their expected role as women-dominating heterosexual men, for relating physically and emotionally with other men in ways that exceed the bounds of heteromale-sanctioned "bonding" or competition, for participating in behavior deemed "feminine" and therefore inferior. Many of us have the option of "passing" as straight men and thereby gaining the male privilege that shields men from the physical and sexual violence inflicted by men on women. In addition, white gay men who pass as heterosexual gain access to positions of social privilege not available to gay men of color. In violence against lesbians, on the other hand, it is impossible to unravel the elements of hatred of lesbians from hatred of women. The phenomenon of lesbians "passing" as straight women provides no parallel to gay men passing as straight men; passing does not shield lesbians of any color from pervasive male violence against women.

2. Lesbian & gay bodies as toxic markers

The bodies of lesbian women and gay men have served as toxic markers by the larger social order, such as in the recently reported higher than average incidence of breast cancer among lesbian women[6] and the heavy toll AIDS takes among gay men of all colors. Here again, paying attention to difference reveals the different patterns of visibility and invisibility that result from the intersection of sexuality, gender, race and class in these social expressions of bodily toxins. While the higher incidence of breast cancer among lesbians has remained virtually invisible in mainstream society and has attracted little attention from medical researchers, AIDS has resulted in a forced visibility of gay men that links gay male identity with violation of the bounds of "natural" sexuality (read: heterosexual monogamy) in order to "blame the victim." Yet this visibility of persons with AIDS has reproduced patterns of exclusion and visibility along lines of race, class, and gender; even as people of color, poor persons, and women increasingly have contracted AIDS, the image of the PWA in mainstream society and among many gay men continues to be affluent white gay men.

The example of health crises in our communities illustrates another of Hunt's points: the typical failure of reciprocity of solidarity by gay men toward lesbians that adds to the male-centeredness of the movement. While gay men understandably have been overwhelmed and preoccupied by the AIDS pandemic, where were we before, and where are we now when women's bodies--and particularly lesbian bodies--were and are on the line? The involvement of lesbians in the AIDS crisis has not been reciprocated by gay men's participation in health issues important to lesbians, whether fighting for abortion rights, against sexual violence against women, or in the fight against breast cancer and other illnesses where society's toxins show up in women's bodies.

3. Lesbian & gay male bodies as markers of pollution & decadence

The recent debate over the participation of lesbians and gay men in the military also reveals dynamics created by the intersection of homophobia and sexism where lesbian and gay bodies become social markers for broader societal debates on gender roles and sexual and relational mores. The debate quickly centered on issues of pollution and decadence: The presence of sexually uncontrollable gay men allegedly threatens the needed order and discipline maintained by compulsory heteromale gender roles. Ironically what is lost on the military leaders who insisted on maintaining the ban was revealed graphically in the beating death of the gay Navy midshipman Allen Schindler: It is not homosexuality but homophobia acted out by heterosexually-identified men that is the ultimate threat to order, discipline, and camaraderie in the military.

The different locations of lesbians and gay men in the military means the combination of sexism and homophobia affects them differently. As in the case of anti-gay and anti-lesbian violence, while gay men must fear anti-gay violence should their sexual orientation be revealed, lesbians face sexual harassment, threats of violence, and denial of opportunities for professional advancement *as women* whether or not they are revealed as lesbian. This is compounded by lesbian-baiting that accompanies sexual harassment and the threat of exposure should lesbians--or any women--refuse male sexual advances. Attention to these and other differences between lesbian and gay male experience is critical for understanding how to respond to the issue of lesbian women and gay men working in the military in the face of officially-sanctioned persecution and implicitly accepted hostility.

Hunt's critique of collapsing lesbian and gay male experience into a single unit is especially apt here: virtually overnight the issue was labeled "Gays in the military" and nearly all the public controversy centered on the danger of having gay male bodies intermingled with (presumably) heterosexual male bodies--in showers, in bunkhouses, in foxholes. This pathological attention to gay men serves to perpetuate lesbian invisibility and obscure the actual ongoing dynamics of anti-lesbian and anti-gay witch-hunts and expulsions where service-wide lesbians are three times more likely to be expelled than gay men, and six times more likely in the Marine Corps.[7] Gay men who engage in political and ethical analysis of issues such as this one must be acutely aware of the intersection of sexism and homophobia for how it affects lesbian women and gay men in different and similar ways.[8]

4&5. Gay male bodies as social markers of gender: drag & leathersexuality

Gay male practices involving cross-dressing (drag) and hypermasculine expressions such as leathersexuality have served to blur, bend, and extend gender boundaries and roles that uphold compulsory heterosexual complementarity. They have been critically important to many gay men in helping to break through years of heteromale socialization and internalized self-hatred for not conforming to expected masculine roles. They also have generated controversy and debate within gay male circles. Examining these practices from a profeminist commitment reveals a further ambiguous dimension to the way they function in lesbian and gay male circles.

Carter Heyward notes that "It is difficult for lesbians to interpret gay male 'camp' as anything but offensive when it is played out by men who are either ignorant of, or indifference to, the ravages of sexism."[9] Yet, Gary Comstock writes of how important drag was in building noncompetitive community with other gay men that challenged inherited patterns of masculinity. He notes: "As that which is usually considered masculine relaxed, that which is usually thought of as feminine was affirmed. Those ways of thinking, acting, feeling, and being affectionate that had not happened in our biological families happened here. We learned that each of us at early ages had learned to pretend and act our ways through childhood and high school. ...There was no need to guard speech, to keep secrets, to be cautious or ashamed. We also ventured to be silly and marvelous." He describes going in drag to a party together: "With excitement and nervousness we all went in dresses--not to mock or imitate women but to stop mocking ourselves, to stop worshipping the trappings and security of divisions that precisely define maleness and femaleness. We came alive; we were animated; we had so much fun that the demons fled. We slew the dragon that restricts adornment."[10]

Both Heyward's and Comstock's perspectives are valid. They illustrate Hunt's contention that a deep lack of mutual understanding still divides our communities, resulting in practices and interpretations of practices that further polarize us. This was further illustrated in an experience in the Lesbian, Gay, and Bisexual Caucus at Union Theological Seminary in 1992. An incident around the appropriateness of using male drag in worship revealed drastically different interpretations of drag along gender lines. It led to some deeply honest, angry and painful conversation. Some of the gay men were able to explain how drag enabled them to reclaim a feminine side that had literally been beaten out of them as boys. Some of the lesbians in turn were able to articulate how they felt mocked and objectified as women when they saw men in drag parading female clothing that they as women had experienced as anything but liberating. It made us realize how critically important this kind of conversation --exploring our different experiences and different perspectives--is *before* coming together to work on something as controversial as drag.

Similar critiques have been made of gay male leathersexuality as inhumane and misogynist in developing and acting out ritualized practices of hypermasculinity drawn from patriarchal gender roles and values. Gay theologian J. Michael Clark, in contrast, argues that leathersexuality has the potential to subvert unconscious patriarchal power constructs through reflective ritual play: "Ritualistic leathersex shifts dominance and submission, power and pain, from the unreflective realm of social interactions and power hierarchies into a controlled arena, at once turning roles inside out and shattering the facades of everyday human power abuses. ...The rituals of leathersex employ assumed and exaggerated roles to disconnect participants from dayworld reality, not as an escape, but as a route to deepened understanding."[11]

Carter Heyward picks up on this in suggesting that profeminist gay men can teach lesbians "about how playing sexually with power is *not* necessarily to collude with patriarchal principles of domination and control. It can be a way of embodying some profoundly sacred tensions."[12] The key here is combining gay male erotic power play with a feminist sensitivity and commitment to examine the consequences of gay male sexual practices on women. This again requires listening deeply to each other about the experiences and interpretations of meaning we furnish as we seek to find ways to work together. For gay men it means an ongoing search to find ways to affirm the erotic in our lives, to avoid scape-goating both masculinity and women while we create new models of masculinity that honor and affirm both men's and women's experience.[13]

The above discussion of the different ways lesbian and gay male bodies inscribed as social markers are affected by the intersection of homophobia and sexism (as well as racism and classism) is meant to be illustrative rather than exhaustive. In light of it and the insights raised by Hunt and Heyward we can reflect further on the particularities of gay male experiences and how these can guide our interactions with lesbian women and with each other in the shared praxis for justice.

Hunt and Heyward's challenge to gay men's participation in patriarchy reminds us that the fundamental sin of white supremacist, capitalist patriarchy lies in its insistence that men only need women and children--and plants and animals and all other living things--in order to fulfill our lives as patriarchs. Thus all men who work to change ourselves, and thus to change the world, must be accountable to women, children, and the rest of creation whose interests and health men have so long ignored while maintaining male domination. In our conversations we realized that we had developed a criterion for evaluating which men we can trust --trust with our lives, trust with the lives of children (our own and others'), trust with the lives of all we hold dear, trust, indeed, with the world--namely, what is the nature of their concrete, active, daily commitment to the well-being of women, children, and the earth? The relatively few men in our lives with whom we trust everything are those whose lives demonstrate a high level of investment to such a commitment--and that also demonstrate a keen awareness that commitment to the well-being of gay men (and all men) entails a simultaneous commitment to the well-being of women, children, and our whole earth community.

We call this commitment "anti-domination" because it requires men's active resistance to the forces--most often led and defined by men more powerful than ourselves--whose agenda depends on relations of domination and subordination, relations in which some men *enjoy* the "natural" advantage over other men, and nearly all men retain some degree of access to the structured power to dominate women and children. This commitment to anti-domination, to the well-being of all women and children and non-human creation carries within it a necessary, fundamental corollary: a commitment by men of greater privilege and power--white men, for example--to the well-being of those men with less.

Adherence to anti-domination carries consequences for our work, one of which is violating the deeply internalized lesson of not making other men, especially men of our race and class, "look bad." We have found, therefore, that while we read many texts by men, we choose to rely on relatively few. Instead, from our experience of being excluded as gay men and awareness of the exclusion of others because of gender, race, class and nationality, we generally bring a hermeneutic of suspicion to our reading of theological texts, and works in all fields, by men. Certainly, writings by feminists and other women make no claim to be perfect, and a critical approach to *all* texts is a necessary part of liberationist work. Yet, we find our work is most authentic when our engagement with feminist, mujerista, and womanist texts begins with a hermeneutic of appreciation and our initial engagement with texts by men is informed by a hermeneutic of suspicion. We find that increasingly we can reverse this method with texts by men--particularly those by gay- or bi-identified men of all colors and other men of color on whose work we have learned most to rely. But again, these texts are most useful, most trustworthy, when they demonstrate an anti-domination methodology and substance, e.g., when they are explicitly pro-feminist, pro-womanist, anti-racist, etc.[14]

As we have stressed throughout this paper, gay men are not a monolithic social category. At the same time, we understand, as is pointed out by Heyward and Hunt, that to women who experience gay men in the church or in the academy this statement is open to challenge. Still, we have found it critical to our work as white gay men to recognize explicitly that gay men do come in every color, religion, occupation, class, region, ethnicity, and sexuality.[15] This is no mere point of pedantry, because crucial to achieving any substantial and sustainable concrete change in the lives of women and men is understanding and affirming not only the complexities of relations between women and men and relations among women, but also *relations among men* (including relations among *gay* men). Achieving some level of understanding of all three sets of relations, and the relations among those relations, is essential to overcoming patriarchal systems of domination.[16]

In common usage the appellation "gay male" really means *white* gay men (the racial signifier is omitted because it is assumed), and "black men" really means *straight* black men (the sexual signifier is similarly omitted); i.e., if one means "black gay men," one must say so explicitly.[17] This usage does not mean that there are no black men in "the gay community" or no gay men in "the black community," but rather that the interests of the dominant men (white or straight) in each group (gay or black) *appear* to be served by assuming and "naming" (by omission), the absence of men who are "different" from the norm. Of course, such usage involves more than making lists; over and over again, in "the gay (male) community," for example, intense discussions are conducted and important decisions are made about "our" lives as if no person of color shared "our" sexual interests and desire for liberation, i.e., is a member of "our" community.

In light of their continuing invisibility in the "lesbian, gay, and bisexual community," lesbian women of all colors may view the heterogeneity of gay men as a side issue, especially when that invisibility is in large measure sustained by gay men who remain unable, and in too many cases unwilling, to learn how to share power or resources in "our" community's projects and organizations. The perennial unwillingness of gay men to work with lesbian women in political organizations in "our" community is beyond factual dispute. Many gay men simply seem unable to either imagine or practice power-sharing with lesbian women, especially when their "critical mass" reaches some magical number at which the men experience discomfort. Indeed, to rework a telling phrase from black women, in coalition work between gay men and lesbian women, "all the gays are white, all the blacks are men, but only the lesbian is brave."[18]

Thus our commitment to anti-domination includes exposing the *intellectual and moral fraud* in articles or books by gay men which purport to represent gay/lesbian or lesbian/gay experiences, theologies, or worldviews in ways which perpetuate an ideology that lesbian women are a subcategory of gay men, and that all gay men are white. This ideology takes several forms. Some white gay male authors make the bald claim of representing both men and women while actually ignoring the realities of lesbians. Few if any even mention the existence of gay men of color, or of any other difference, since they assume all men are "gay" in the same way. Others perpetuate invisibility with more subtlety by quoting (or using and not quoting) many lesbians and other feminists and womanists (especially Audre Lorde, Alice Walker, and other women of color) *to support their view of the oppression of gays (white men)* while ignoring the central claims and particularities of these women's writings.

Still others claim they can't "represent" lesbians, but then employ universalizing language which results in lumping "all of us" together. This strategy of non-representation parallels what María Lugones calls "non-interactive acknowledgment," the practice which permits the writer from the dominant social location to avoid interacting with the other by acknowledging difference and then ignoring it.[19] As Lugones contends, disclaiming the difference, refusing to engage it, leaves the "other" reader outside the discourse and the normative reader comfortably inside it. Any responsibility for correction lies with the other on the outside, and allows the writer to avoid responsibility for the effects of his social location. Of course, men can't *represent* lesbians, nor white men represent men of color; but we can take their lives, their theologies, seriously enough to stop erasing them.

However, ending erasure is only the first, albeit necessary, move toward what Lugones calls "the interactive step."[20] She is writing explicitly about the encounter between white feminists and feminists of color, wherein many of the former see and name a "problem of difference" as regards the latter. Hers is a very subtle analysis of the various "tricks" racism plays on many white women as they wrestle with this "problem" (which is not the same as wrestling with "difference" itself). Sexism is not identical with racism, of course, but white gay men can learn much about our processes of domination and erasure with lesbians and all women, and also with men of color, from her analysis.[21]

We raise Lugones' point about "the interactive step" to point out where white gay men must move ourselves, that is, to the place where we self-consciously check, at the door, our deeply internalized impulse to universalize our experience, our selves, as we also begin the slow, arduous process of *particularizing* not only ourselves but all the others we have named as Other, and *relating mutually* to those others. Men, *including gay men,* are no longer the teachers "by right of penis," but learners by rite of participation in humanity. We can undertake this interaction only *after* we become clear that there is "the problem of difference" both among us as gay men, *and* also in our relations with out lesbian "sisters" and women generally.[22]

What "our interactive step" requires is that once we recognize these differences we shall have to *engage* those whose difference has been created, largely by *us* and our forbears, in order to define and contain *them.* Engagement will mean taking lesbians, all women, all children, the earth, and all men of less privilege and power seriously enough *to be changed by them.* The experience of feminists of all colors tells us that there is much pain in this process, and that the men who most need to change generally will be the most resistant. In our experience, men often whine and don't accept criticism well, especially from those they thought were safely colonized. Most gay men, white men, have considerable change ahead of us, so we must *expect trauma.* Indeed, men generally have to learn to take most of the world seriously, to be changed self-consciously by it--not only the entire half or more which is female, but also for many of us all the male Others we have, at best, ignored, and, at worst, eliminated. With all this work to do, we hope for the day when the din of change is very loud, for it will mean better days ahead.

There is no guarantee, of course, that women will recognize the work we do, because, frankly, there is no requirement that doing justice (which is rarely simple or easy) be rewarded by anything other than its own fruits. We should expect no plaques, no testimonial dinners--after all, how many have we given for women lately? Instead, what we should expect and demand of one another is concrete engagement to end injustice, to overcome domination and to inaugurate the kin-dom of God in which all God's people experience embodied justice and pleasured embodiment.

In the meantime, we must remember that oppression, like justice, is always embodied. Gay men and lesbian women, and all women and all men *under*powered by *over*-powering men, experience oppression in our bodies. We carry its weight in our limbs, feel its knots in the pits of our stomachs, feel its ache in our heads, feel its soreness in our joints and muscles. Therefore, we submit that the concrete signs of change in our relations with women, children, animals and each other will also be revealed by bodies, our own as well as the bodies of others. How we care for our bodies, and the bodies of others--how our bodies interact--is a clear statement of our commitment to the well-being of all living beings. What is antithetical to our well-being, and the well-being of so many others, is to perpetuate structures which maintain and strengthen the domination of some bodies by other, "more worthy" bodies. What is required is that we put our bodies on the line for "anti-domination," and that includes ending our complicity as bodies who dominate.

For example, where we put our bodies on the line *politically* matters because it can reveal the particularities of our commitment to concrete action for justice. In April 1993, both of us went to Washington, DC, to march for lesbian, gay, bisexual and transgender rights and liberation. In April 1992, we both made a different decision with our bodies. We did not go to Washington to march for reproductive freedom for women (and us all). We both send money to women's advocacy groups such as NOW and NARAL, but our bodies were not on the line for women struggling to retain the right to an abortion. Putting our whole bodies on *that* line--not just our check-writing hands--would serve as an invitation to others as well. There is a leavening effect of bodies joined together for justice--each body on the line, more than taking up space, actually encourages other bodies to join, too. Therefore, the interactive step requires that men put our bodies on the line politically for women.

Few gay men we know fail to have more than one friend who is (whose body is) HIV+ or AIDS-symptomatic. How those who are HIV- put their bodies on the line, literally, with friends as well as strangers is very revealing of our political/spiritual praxis, of our ability to be compassionate, to *be passionate with* those we love who are struck by this awful plague. Alas, some men are unable to hug or kiss HIV+ friends or friends with AIDS. Others just stop seeing their friends who are sick. We know embodying AIDS-passion is difficult; we *want* to work with those who are concretely, daily living with AIDS. What we too often want to forget, however, is that we, too, are living with AIDS. Too often, therefore, we don't put our bodies on that line. The interactive step requires that men put our bodies on the line politically for *men, women, children, and the earth.*

Where we put our bodies on the line *relationally* matters, too. The identities of our friends and lovers can be an indication of how well we embody values of inclusivity and justice. The interactive step requires us to learn to *notice* people we like, including those who are people of a different color or able-ness, to actually *look* at them as people, to *listen* to the stories they tell of their lives, to *see* them as individuals not as members of minority groups, to *respond* with integrity out of our own lives, to *share* our feelings, to *take time* to "be" with them, to *resist* the temptation to sexualize them (especially if they are men), while also not robbing them of their sexuality and sexual uniqueness--in short, to make friends by offering ourselves as friends and accepting their friendliness as it is offered in return.

For both of us children are an integral and inseparable part of our lives--as a father, as godfathers, as uncles, as friends. We are acutely aware how many gay men use the derisive term "breeders" to describe people who have children. Both of us are considering raising a child from infancy with another man because we yearn to share the care for a child with a male partner. Many men share our feelings. Every gay man who is able to separate his anger at heterosexism from persons who seem to represent heterosexist hegemony (from the children they produce), has made a major gain in embodying connectedness among us all. Our interactive step requires us to be open to friendly, caring relationships with all sorts of people of any race, sex, sexual preference, or age--as well as with nonhuman creatures.

Where we put our bodies on the line *spiritually* matters, too. For us, as for many other gay men, body adornment and clothing are not only matters of fashion, but also spiritual practices. As we indicated above, we are aware that many feminists find male "camp" or "drag" problematic, as do we when it mocks women or expresses misogyny.

Others of us, however, practice it spiritually, as a way to pleasure our bodies. Soft, silky fabrics feel good against our skin, just as the lack of binding when we wearing a skirt allows air to circulate freely around our genitals which also hang easily when not encased in pants and underwear. Imaginatively decorating our faces and wearing jewelry express our inner beauty. These are ways to feel, to experience the pleasure of our bodies differently, to embody aspects of our freer spirits.

Frankly, often when we wear a jacket and tie--that is, dress in the conventional male professional mode--we feel *dis*embodied, "out of our bodies," and we realize that *that* is true "cross-dressing," that is, dressing against ourselves. Interactively embodied spirituality requires men's sensitivity to women's concerns as it also leads us to ask them to listen with keen ears and look with keen eyes to discern our various types of spiritual costuming. Perhaps we all will be able to identify our respective stakes in refusing complicity in the fashion systems which manipulate and control our bodies.

Where we put our bodies on the line *sexually* matters as well. Some months ago Robin went to a gay male sex club, what is called a "j.o." or "jerk-off club." He noted that "There were many bodies, all of them naked, and most of them beautiful by very conventional standards. As far as I could tell, 'safe sex' was practiced by everyone. In that way, we put our bodies on the line for life. However, I didn't experience much life being shared. No one talked. When I asked one man what the 'etiquette' was I quickly learned it included no communication other than the mechanics of sex. There was eye contact, but no one *really looked* deeply. I could see no desire for connection, except one man's hand to another man's penis. There wasn't any laughter, or a smile of pleasure, even when a large group of men merged into a mass of sexual action. Of course, after a while the absurdity of it all made me want to laugh. And cry."

We recognize that there is a spectrum of gay male sexual practices, and that many group sexual experiences--including "recreational sex" which does not encompass the expectation of, or even desire for, longer-term commitment --do include authentic human communication, and ongoing friendship and relationship with the other men involved. For example, Robin has experienced this authenticity in the "back room" of his favorite East Village bar in New York City. Yet, we have learned that one place not to put our bodies is where sex is competitive, judgmental, or controlled by rigid rules which prohibit the possibility of interaction at *all* the deepest levels.

Robin recalls Radical Faerie gatherings as one such place of real sexual pleasure--where men touch *and* talk, where men smile before, during, and after orgasm, where laughter is likely to be mixed with deep groanings of pleasure. "I remember a gathering several years ago where a dozen or so men were having sex, in pairs and larger groupings, while several other men sat nearby telling jokes and puns--sometimes dreadful, sometimes wickedly funny humor which brought groans, or chuckles, or real laughter, not only from the other jokesters but also from those of us writhing on the floor. I am grateful, delighted, to put my body on that line." Our interactive embodiment requires that we have fun while passionately violating the anti-sodomy laws of 26 states and generally making much of the world very uncomfortable. How else will we know we're making love if we don't laugh (and even cry)?

In the final analysis, our ability to communicate through difference among us as gay men, and through difference with our lesbian sisters, will turn on our ability to take not only our own bodies seriously but also theirs with equal seriousness. Putting our bodies on the line for women's reproductive health, for the struggle against breast cancer and AIDS, for safer sex, for the rights and well-being of those oppressed by white supremacy, for the rights and well-being of children, for spirituality grounded in and affirmative of our bodies, for sex which promotes connection, for an end to gendered tyrannies of fashion and patriarchal structures and roles which oppress, as well as for items not mentioned above--for work with dignity and adequate compensation for all people, for universal health care, for housing which shelters every body decently and safely, for mental health care understood to be embodied care--for all this and more, our bodies--where we put them, how we display them, how we connect them with others, how much heavy lifting we are prepared to do for others as well as ourselves--will say more than all the words we can write.

Struggling for justice means embodying justice. Gay men embody justice by where we put our penises and our other organs of pleasure. We also embody justice by where we plant our feet and refuse to be moved, how we raise our arms laden with a placard demanding justice and open our mouths to shout resistance to hatred, or put our hands to wipe a feverish brow or hold the hand of a child in our own hand. *The pleasure of justice, the justice of pleasure, belong to us, reside in our bodies, but only as we share this justice, this pleasure, with all the bodies in the world.* Embodying justice, embodying pleasure, means living not in the splendid isolation of patriarchs but rather in embodied connections--as if our bodies depend on others' and theirs depend on ours--as indeed *we* do.

---

[1]Unless noted otherwise, "we" in this paper refers to the shared claims and commitments of the two authors. We speak from the particularities of our own locations and experiences, and do not presume to speak for other gay men or lesbian women. We do, however, take seriously the experiences others have articulated, and are grateful for this opportunity to join our voices in the conversation.

[2]See Shira Maguen, "Teen Suicide: The Government's Cover-up and America's Lost Children," *The Advocate*, No. 586 (September 24, 1991), 40-47.

[3]Ellen Herman, "Getting to Serenity: Do Addiction Programs Sap Our Political Vitality?" *Outlook*, Vol. 1, No. 2 (Summer, 1988), 10-18.

[4]See "Organizing Against Violence," *The 1993 New York Pride Guide* (New York: Pride Publishers, Inc., 1993), 21.

[5]John Gallagher, "A Month of Hate: An Epidemic of Violence," *The Advocate*, Issue 589 (November 5, 1991), 42-48.

[6]For a helpful summary of the statistics on breast cancer in lesbian women and the debate around their interpretation, see Tatiana Schreiber, "One in Three? Lesbians and Breast Cancer." *The 1993 New York Pride Guide* (New York: Pride Publications, Inc., 1993), 114.

[7]See "A (Quiet) Uprising in the Ranks," *Newsweek* (June 21, 1993), 60.

[8]The complex dynamics of race in this debate are revealing. The invisibility of race among lesbian and gay male members of the military (which furthers the stereotype that all lesbian women and gay men are white) stands in marked contrast to the vehemence with which officers of all colors in the military denied any parallel between the current effort to overturn the ban on homosexuals in the military and President Truman's act to end racial segregation in the armed forces by race following World War II. The quick effort of many white gay men and lesbians to draw on this experience also was controversial in the African American community and exposed the complex dynamics of appropriating the historical experiences of a different community for one's own ends. These dynamics are explored further below.

[9]Carter Heyward, "Embodying the Connections," 9.

[10]Gary David Comstock, *Gay Theology Without Apology* (Cleveland: Pilgrim, 1993), 18.

[11]J. Michael Clark, "Leathersexuality," *Theologizing Gay: Fragments of Liberation Activity*, (Oakcliff, TX: Minuteman Press, 1991), 17-18.

[12]Heyward, "Embodying the Connections," 11.

[13]Another question about leathersexuality arises from an ecological perspective. If gay men take seriously the ecological demand that we expand our community of accountability to include animals and the whole earth community, it may also mean questioning the connection of our integrated erotic spirituality and sexuality to wearing leather which involves us as participants in the "trafficking of animal corpses" for human gratification. For an ecofeminist analysis of "trafficking in animals" and the animal industry, see Carol Adams, "The Feminist Traffic in Animals," *Ecofeminism: Women, Animals, Nature*, Greta Gaard, ed. (Philadclphia: Temple University Press, 1993), 195-218.

[14]On the other hand we are learning to enjoy reading imaginative literature by men, because so often we find "men of difference" in them who, if only in modest ways, offer models of resistance to patriarchal domination.

[15]We are moving toward an understanding of gay men that sees "us" occupying many "sexual spaces" that blur conventional boundaries denoted by dichotomized sexual identities such as straight and gay.

[16]For an exposition of the links among homosexuality, homophobia/biphobia and patriarchy, see Elias Farajaje-Jones, "Breaking Silence: Toward an In-the-Life Theology," *Black Theology: A Documentary History. Volume Two: 1980-1992,* James Cone and Gayraud Wilmore, eds. (Maryknoll, NY: Orbis, 1993), 139-159. For a longer, more theoretical, and classic treatment, see Beverly Harrison, "Misogyny and Homphobia: The Unexplored Connections," in *Making the Connections: Essays in Feminist Social Ethics*, Carol Robb, ed. (Boston: Beacon Press, 1985), 135-151.

[17]The same dynamic is apparent in references to men in other racial/ethnic groups. Hence "Hispanic men" or "Asian men" or "Native American men" means *straight* men in these groups; one must add the signifier "gay" or "bisexual" to include different sexualities.

[18]Gloria T. Hull, Patricia Bell Scott, and Barbara Smith, eds., *All the Women are White, All the Blacks are Men, But Some of Us Are Brave: Black Women's Studies* (New York: Feminist Press at the City University of New York, 1982).

[19]María C. Lugones, "On the Logic of Pluralist Feminism," in *Feminist Ethics*, Claudia Card, ed. (Lawrence, KS: University of Kansas Press, 1991), 38.

[20]*Ibid.*, 39.

[21]James Baldwin makes a similar point about race when he writes "whatever white people do not know about Negroes reveals, precisely and inexorably, what they do not know about themselves." James Baldwin, "The Fire Next Time," in *The Price of the Ticket* (New York: St. Martin's Press, 1985), 350.

[22]We would like to think gay men can move directly to engaging "difference" without first setting up "the problem of difference," but our own struggles incline us to the view that male supremacy and white supremacy are so powerful that we shall have to spend considerable time at this problematizing step.

Notes on Contributors

Julie Byrne, originally from Annville, PA, is a doctoral candidate in the Program in Religion, Culture and Critical Theory at Duke University, Durham, NC. Her dissertation engages works by Catholic authors and artists to modify leftist critiques of capitalism.

J. Michael Clark is an itinerant academic and co-founder of the Gay Men's Issues in Religion Group of the American Academy of Religion, serving as its co-chair 1987-1993. He lives with his spouse, Bob McNeir, and their ecosystem of dogs, birds, fishpond, flower and vegetable gardens on a hill overlooking downtown Atlanta. Author of a dozen books in gay studies, his most recent book is *Beyond our Ghettos: Gay Theology in Ecological Perspective* (Pilgrim Press, 1993). The present essay appeared in a different context and format as "(Em)Body(d) Theology: Exploring Ecology and Eschatology," *Journal of Men's Studies*, 3.1 (August 1994), and is reprinted herein with permission.

Robin Gorsline is a doctoral candidate at Union Theological Seminary, New York, whose research interests include queer theory and anti-white supremacy studies and their relation to religion. He is also a queer dad who looks fabulous in pearls--the proud parent of three children, including a daughter who lives with him in Brooklyn (who gave him the pearls!).

Ronald E. Long, an adjunct assistant professor in the Program in Religion, Hunter College (CUNY), has also taught at Columbia and Vassar. A graduate of Kenyon College, he received his doctorate from Columbia and was a Fulbright scholar in Germany. He focuses on issues of fundamental theology in light of the problem of natural evil and on issues in ethics and spirituality arising from gay experience He has written *AIDS, God, and Faith* (with J. Michael Clark), as well as numerous articles in the *Journal of Men's Studies.* He is currently developing a book-length study, tentatively entitled "Re-membering the Body: Wisdom from the Gay Ghetto." Considerable portions of the present essay appeared in a different context and format as "An Affair of Men: Masculinity and the Dynamics of Gay Sex," *Journal of Men's Studies*, 3.1 (August 1994), and is reprinted herein with permission.

Daniel T. Spencer was born and raised in California; he received his B.A. in geology (1979) from Carleton College, Northfield, MN, and his M.Div. (1983) from Union Theological Seminary, New York. He served as Director of Latin American Programs (1984-1989) at the Center for Global Education, Augsburg College, Minneapolis, taking groups interested in justice and human rights issues to Latin America. He completed a Ph.D. in Christian Ethics at Union Theological Seminary in 1994; his dissertation, *Gay and Gaia: A Liberationist Contribution to Ecological Ethics*, combines ecological and liberationist insights and methodological issues to outline an ecological ethic grounded in contemporary liberation theologies. He is currently Assistant Professor of Religion, Drake University, Des Moines.